JOHN GALSWORTHY

Strife

With Commentary and Notes by
NON WORRALL

D0112270

Methuen Student Editions
METHUEN · LONDON and NEW YORK

This Methuen Student Edition first published in 1984 by
Methuen London Ltd., 11 New Fetter Lane, London EC4P 4EE
and Methuen Inc., 733 Third Avenue, New York, NY 10017

ISBN 0 413 54270 X

Set by ⟁ Tek-Art, Croydon, Surrey
Reproduced, printed and bound in Great Britain by
Hazell Watson & Viney Limited,
Member of the BPCC Group,
Aylesbury, Bucks

Contents

A selection of photographs from the 1978 production at the National Theatre in London appears on pages 63 ff. The play was directed by Christopher Morahan. The photos are by Nobby Clark.

John Galsworthy: 1867-1933

1867   Born 14 August. His family was quite wealthy, his father
being a solicitor and company director. He had two sisters
and one brother. Educated at a small prep. school in
Bournemouth and then at Harrow Public School where he
was considered a reasonable scholar and an excellent athlete.
Read Law at New College, Oxford. A rich, good-looking,
well-dressed student, Galsworthy's academic career was
conventional and undistinguished. He joined the Oxford
University Drama Society (OUDS) and wrote *Guddirore*, a
skit on Gilbert and Sullivan's *Ruddigore*.

1890   Galsworthy was called to the Bar but . . . 'I read in various
Chambers, practised almost not at all and disliked my
profession thoroughly'. He first met Georg Sauter, a
Bavarian artist, whose ideas, so different from those of the
conventional middle-class English family, interested
Galsworthy.

1891   16 July: the first of many trips abroad — to Canada. On his
return he met his future wife, Ada, at a family party to
celebrate her wedding to Major Arthur Galsworthy, John's
cousin.

1892   Travelled in Australasia with a schoolfriend, Ted Sanderson.
  -3   They returned to England on S.S. Torrens, on which they
met the author Joseph Conrad, who was first mate. He
became a life-long friend and adviser to Galsworthy. Back
in England he again met Ada, whose marriage was already
extremely unhappy.

1894   Still undecided about the career in Law envisaged for him
by his father, Galsworthy wished he had '. . . the gift of
writing. I really think that is the nicest way of making
money going, only it isn't really the writing so much as the
thoughts one wants; and when you feel like a very shallow
pond with no nice cool deep pool with queer and pleasant
things at the bottom, what's the good?' (letter to Monica
Sanderson). During this year, as he became more attached
to Ada, he now saw himself 'in chains' to Ada and writing.

1895 Easter: while standing at a bookstall at the Gare du Nord, Ada remarked to Galsworthy: 'Why don.t you write? You're just the person.' Traditionally this is regarded as the remark which made up Galsworthy's mind. By September Galsworthy was Ada's lover. His attitude towards her was intensely romantic, almost chivalric.

1897- First publications under the pseudonym of John Sinjohn:
1901 two novels, *Jocelyn* and *Villa Rubein,* and two volumes of short stories, *From the Far Winds* and *Man of Devon.*

1902 Ada separated from her husband, holidaying abroad each year with John. Progressively, as his affair with her became known, it ensured that he would not be received or regarded as respectable by most of his own class. By this time Galsworthy was a well-established participant at the Literary Lunches held at the Mont Blanc Restaurant, presided over by the critic, Edward Garnett, and also attended by such as Hilaire Belloc, W.H. Hudson, Ford Madox Ford and Joseph Conrad.

February: he sent the first draft of his novel *The Island Pharisees* to Garnett for his comments. This procedure became his usual practice; Galsworthy frequently amended texts extensively on the basis of what friends such as Garnett and Conrad said.

1903 Galsworthy's mother left his father (then aged 86) because she felt he was too fond of his grandchildren's governess.

1904 8 December: his father died after a long and harrowing illness.

1905 No longer worried about the effect of scandal upon his father, John and Ada decided to give grounds for divorce. They travelled abroad throughout the period of the divorce proceedings to avoid unpleasantness and embarrassment. Ada became totally dedicated to John's work, acting as secretary and typist as well as adviser.

23 September: John and Ada married and lived in Galsworthy's house in London.

1906 Termed Galsworthy's 'annus mirabilis' by his biographer, H.V. Marrot. His novel *The Man of Property* was published and received excellent reviews. From this point, Galsworthy was fully established as a writer.

25 September: his first play, *The Silver Box,* was produced by the Vedrenne-Barker management at the Royal Court. The play concerns the stealing of a silver cigarette box from the house of John Barthwick, MP, by Jones, the husband of

the Barthwicks' charlady. He also steals the purse from the handbag of the woman Barthwick's son Jack has been out with and which Jack has 'stolen' from her in fun. The woman comes to claim her property the next morning. The climax of the play is the trial in which Jack's 'theft' is concealed from the court, while the wretched Jones, who has no influential friends or lawyers, is sentenced to imprisonment. Galsworthy supervised the casting, attended all rehearsals and was closely involved with all aspects of the production. This became his usual procedure with the majority of his plays.

1907 Galsworthy joined the campaign against censorship in the theatre which arose from problems surrounding Garnett's play, *The Breaking Point.* He also paid the first of many visits to Dartmoor and other prisons, building up a vivid picture of the horrors of prison life.

24 September: *Joy* was produced at the Savoy Theatre by the Vedrenne-Barker partnership. The play deals with a young girl's disillusionment when she discovers that her adored mother is in love with a 'disreputable bounder' who is more important to her than is her daughter. It was a failure with both critics and audiences.

The Country House, a novel, published.

1908 *A Commentary* published — a collection of articles on a vast number of subjects including censorship in the theatre and solitary confinement. Galsworthy had by this time become the champion of numerous causes.

Spring: the Galsworthys took over the lease of Wingstone Farm on Dartmoor. They spent part of each year there where John felt able to write most freely but, partly because of Ada's rather delicate health, they rarely stayed in one place for long.

1909 9 March: *Strife* was produced at the Duke of York's Theatre. It was a resounding success, the *Evening Standard,* for example, announcing: 'It is the English play for which we have been waiting.'

May: open Letter to Home Secretary, Herbert Gladstone, on the subject of 'separate confinement'.

September: *A Minute on Separate Confinement* — Galsworthy's written account of interviews with a large number of convicts and a summary of the effects of solitary confinement on different types of people. As a result of this, he was interviewed by Gladstone and the term of separate confinement was reduced to a uniform three months for all types of prisoners. *Fraternity* published.

1910   21 February: *Justice* was produced at the Duke of York's Theatre. Within his treatment of the case of Falder who is found guilty of fraud and then destroyed by a system of justice which condemns him to solitary confinement, Galsworthy dramatized what he had seen during his many visits to prisons. The audience's reception of the production was astounding and the play's impact great. Winston Churchill, who had replaced Gladstone as Home Secretary, was so impressed by it that he put into immediate effect certain measures for prison reform including a reduction in the number of hours per day spent 'in solitary'.

1911   *The Little Dream* — an allegorical play with music and dance — was produced in Manchester with Margaret Morris, a vivacious 19-year-old dancer with whom Galsworthy gradually realised he was in love.

1912   Galsworthy became a member of the Academic Committee of the Royal Society of Literature but his personal life was in crisis. Ada's reaction to knowledge of John's involvement with Margaret Morris was so intensely despairing that John decided he could hurt her no further. Travelling in France in February and more extensively in America later in the year provided distractions for them both. America proved a very rewarding audience for Galsworthy's novels and plays. He was in great demand on the lecture circuit.
23 November: *The Eldest Son*, produced at the Kingsway Theatre, deals with the conflict for the baronet's son, Bill Cheshire, arising from an affair with Freda, the lady's maid. Ultimately his political ambitions and the family name are saved by the girl's dignity and altruism in rejecting his offer of marriage thus releasing him from a socially disastrous liaison. According to Ada, this was 'Fairly good "succés d'estime" and the usual commercial failure'.

1913   16 September: *The Fugitive* was performed at the Royal Court Theatre. The critics found this play on the subject of marital unhappiness in which the heroine, Clare Dedmond, commits suicide because of her distress at being married to a man who physically repels her, depressing and lacking in humour.

1914   Productions of *Justice* and *Strife* in Vienna were very warmly received.

4 August: England involved in World War I. Galsworthy's diary reads: 'We are in . . . The horror of the thing keeps coming over one in waves; and all happiness has gone out of life. I can't keep still and I can't work . . . If this war is not the death of Christianity, it will be odd. We need a creed that really applies humanism to life instead of talking of it.' He felt he should volunteer but could not leave Ada. In an attempt to assuage the resultant guilt, he worked tremendously hard to raise relief funds — £1,250 during the first year of the war.

1915   6 May: Galsworthy's mother died.

Georg Sauter, his brother-in-law, was interned as an alien. Galsworthy was furious and distressed.

September: Galsworthy was forced by 'bad headaches' to take a rest from writing. He was exhausted by the constant pressure of work.

1916-   He donated a house in London to the Red Cross as a
1917   Wounded Soldiers' Club along with £400 to refurbish it.

November — March: John and Ada went to work at a convalescent home for wounded soldiers at Die near Valance, France. Ada was in charge of linen and John a masseur. Busy and active, Galsworthy found this the happiest time of the war years.

1918   17 April: Galsworthy was appointed editor of a periodical which he renamed *Reveille*. Three editions of a very high standard resulted with contributors such as Kipling, Barrie, Conrad and Hardy.

Galsworthy was offered a knighthood but declined: '. . . no artist of Letters ought to dally with titles and rewards of that nature' (Diary: 1 January).

17 July: he finally offered himself as a volunteer for the Army Reserve but was granted a certificate of discharge on the grounds of being 'permanently and totally unfit for any form of Military Service', bringing him a tremendous sense of relief that he had not been shirking his duty.

25 July: *Five Tales*, including *The Indian Summer of a Forsyte*, published. At last a return to Galsworthy's high standard of writing.

September: John and Ada moved to Grove Lodge, Hampstead.

11 November: Armistice ends the First World War.

1919   February: in America for Lowell Centenary Celebrations as
the representative of English Literature, Galsworthy gave a
series of lectures.

1920   April: to enormous commercial and critical acclaim, *The
Skin Game* appeared at St Martin's Theatre. Here the
question is whether it is right for the 'nouveau riche'
Hornblower family to build a factory in such a position
that it will spoil the view from the house of the
representatives of landed gentry, the Hillcrist family.
Although Galsworthy's output was as prolific as usual (the
novels, *In Chancery* and *Awakening,* were both published
that year), in a letter to Dorothy Easton in September, he
wrote: 'I feel absolutely without hope of ever writing
anything worth reading again.'

1921   Galsworthy became the First President of the Founding
Centre of the International PEN Club, an office which he
held until his death.
To Let, the first part of The Forsyte Saga, published.

1922   8 March: *Loyalties* was produced at St Martin's Theatre.
During the course of a house party, a guest, De Levis (a
social climber and a Jew) accuses Dancy (popular ex-army
hero) of stealing a thousand pounds from his room. Public
opinion is entirely on Dancy's side but he is proved guilty
and shoots himself. This play was highly praised by the
critics. The *Sunday Times* insisted it was '. . . almost
entitled to rank as a classic of its kind'. Galsworthy became
Hon. Professor of Dramatic literature of the Royal Society
of Literature.

1924   3 August: Conrad died and in October Galsworthy suffered
further grief when his sister, Lilian, died.
The White Monkey, first part of a trilogy about Fleur,
daughter of Soames Forsyte, published.

1926   12 August: at the Ambassadors Theatre, *Escape* ran very
successfully for a year. It is a play about a young man who
accidentally kills a policeman because he unjustly accused a
prostitute of soliciting, and who escapes from the injustice
of the Law.
The Silver Spoon published.
The Galsworthys moved to Bury House in Sussex.
Galsworthy proved an excellent landlord, paying small
private pensions to particularly impoverished families and
building well-equipped cottages for his staff.

1928 *Swan Song* published.

1929 The Order of Merit was conferred upon Galsworthy.

1931 August: Galsworthy suffered his first attack of loss of speech. In November he underwent a course of radium treatment. As the symptoms of his illness became more apparent and debilitating, Galsworthy still could not accept the fact that he was ill.

1932 Galsworthy continued to force himself to write. 10 December: he was awarded the Nobel Prize for Literature but was too ill to travel to Stockholm to receive it. He gave the prize money of £9,000 in Trust to PEN Club.

1933 31 January: Galsworthy died and was cremated. A memorial service was held at Westminster Abbey. His ashes were scattered on the hills above Bury by his nephew as he had requested.

Plot

Act I

At noon on February 7, the Board of the Trenartha Tin Plate Company (situated on the Welsh Border) meets at the house of the works manager, Francis Underwood. A strike has been in progress throughout the winter; in an effort to settle the issue the Board, many of whose members are English and live in London, have come to discuss the situation with the men and their Union representative.

The differences in attitude of the various Board members are made apparent in the opening dialogue. Wanklin and Wilder, supported more half-heartedly by Scantlebury, desire a compromise with the men over their demands, fearing the effects which a prolonged strike would have on the size of the dividend that the Company would be able to pay its shareholders. Edgar Anthony, the Chairman's son, sees the Board's intransigence as cruelty, while his father, John Anthony, regards any suggestion of compromise as weakness. Although in theory they all agree with the Chairman that they should *not* give in, in practice they would all prefer to settle with the men and end the dispute.

With the appearance of Harness, the Union official, the Board draws together as if against a common enemy. Harness is told by Anthony that the Board will not make any concessions; the other members remain silent. At Scantlebury's suggestion, a delegation of five strikers is brought in. Their leader, Roberts, expects the Board to make an offer; when one is not forthcoming he turns to leave, the others following as if hypnotised. When Harness attempts to establish a dialogue between the two sides, the personal opposition between Anthony and Roberts becomes obvious, each seeing it as a trial of strength to prove who is master. Division amongst the strikers is emphasised by Thomas's unsuccessful attempts to put his view — attempts which are sarcastically quashed by Roberts. Finally at Anthony's behest, Roberts explains the men's position. They want their demands to be met in full and will not be starved into submission. Anthony reiterates that not a single demand will be granted and adjourns the meeting until five o'clock. The men leave, together with Harness.

Enid, Underwood's wife, enters to announce that lunch is
served, prompting a general exodus with the exception of
Anthony, her father. She takes the opportunity to attempt to
change her father's mind by emphasising the distress the strike is
causing to women and children and in particular to Annie, now
married to Roberts but previously Enid's maid. Her father refuses
to be moved, giving as his reason the effect such compromises
would eventually have on the culture and comforts of the middle
class. Enid then tries to make him change his mind by drawing his
attention to the effect such stress could have on his own delicate
health, but Anthony remains adamant.

As Enid leaves impatiently, Tench, Secretary to the Board,
enters, requesting Anthony to sign some documents. He makes it
clear to his employer that not only does he wish for a compromise
but that the Directors are going to overturn the ruling of the
Chairman. Even this cannot make Anthony change his mind.
After Frost, the butler, has brought Anthony a whisky and soda
and made his own enquiry as to the worth of a strike which
causes strain and ill-health to his master, Anthony is left alone on
the stage.

Act II Scene I
At 3.30 the same afternoon in the kitchen of Roberts' cottage,
Annie Roberts and a group of other strikers' wives are seated
around a meagre fire. There is neither money nor food and the
women are hungry and cold. Despite their suffering they seem to
accept the reasons for the strike with the exception of Madge
Thomas who, as the others leave, launches a vociferous attack on
Roberts, blaming him alone for the fact that the men are still
holding out. She insists that in their hearts all the men are against
Roberts but are too cowardly to make a stand against him.

A tapping at the door heralds the entrance of Enid who wants
to know why Annie has returned the food she sent. When Enid
blames Roberts for all the suffering, Madge insists that there is
none, accusing Enid of spying. Madge leaves, angrily instructing
Enid not to visit her house. Once on their own, it is obvious that
Annie and Enid are fond of each other, but each woman thinks the
other should persuade her own menfolk to act sensibly. Both have
a deeply engrained sense of loyalty, Annie to her husband, Enid to
her father. Enid's attempts to make Annie think that Roberts and
the working men are to blame for the terrible living conditions the

women have to endure fail miserably; the class barriers are too strong to be broken by individual acts of kindness.

As Roberts's footsteps are heard outside, his wife tries to avoid a confrontation by asking Enid to leave. Enid stays to make her own appeal to Roberts to come to some compromise for his wife's sake. Roberts, insisting that Enid really wants a compromise for her father's sake, turns her arguments back on her by accusing her father of condemning the women and children to such deprivation. Their argument causes Annie physical distress. As Roberts turns away to cut some bread as if dismissing Enid, Mr. Underwood arrives to collect his wife. With her last appeal rejected, Enid leaves with her husband.

Roberts shows concern for his wife by wrapping his overcoat around her, telling her that there is no fight in any of the Directors apart from Anthony but that there is no heart in the men either. Annie puts the case for the women, who Roberts thinks should put up with the consequences although they have no power of decision about the strike. He is convinced that the Directors are on the point of defeat, but as he leaves to attend the strike meeting, refusing to take his overcoat which is keeping her warm, he cannot meet his wife's eyes — he knows he must share the responsibility for her state of health.

On his way out, he passes a young lad, Jan Thomas, who tells Annie that his father and sister are on their way to the cottage. It transpires that Thomas, largely because of his religious beliefs, is convinced that a compromise must be reached and wished to persuade Roberts of the same before he addressed the meeting. As he goes off to the meeting, his daughter, Madge, passes him in the doorway and Rous, another striker and Madge's lover, enters hurriedly behind her. Madge and Rous are in the middle of an argument, she urging him to compromise, he emphasising that he promised to stand by Roberts. When Rous finally rushes off to the meeting, Madge knows that her attraction for and power over him will ensure that he votes against Roberts.

Madge suddenly realises that Annie, who has observed all this, has sunk back into her chair. Obviously extremely ill, she recovers and leans forward excitedly despite her pain as she hears the sounds of the strikers gathering for the meeting.

Act II Scene II

Past four o'clock in a grey failing light, the scene changes to the strikers' meeting. Harness is standing on the makeshift platform having just finished addressing the men. Following questions about the Board's employment of strikebreakers, he continues to reinforce the Union's point that the men should be prepared to reduce their demands in line with Union policy so that the Union can feel justified in taking up their case. Having specifically isolated the furnace men's demands as being excessive, Harness leaves the men to make their decision. Roberts stands alone as the men close up in groups to discuss their position. The question of the women's reaction is raised and Thomas yells a demand that the delegation be given the power to compromise. Thrust on to the platform, the old Welshman's case is that they have been beaten by Nature and should take their beating like men. He distrusts the Union which has done nothing to help him in the twenty five years he has paid his dues. The men should act on their own behalf and make peace with the Board.

Jago, an engineer, representing the group of workers whose demands the Union wishes to separate from the majority, speaks out against dividing their claims, accusing those who desire this of being out to save their own skins. This causes restlessness and embarrassment in the crowd. Rous now addresses the men, arguing the Union's case in favour of compromise rather than continuing to starve women and children.

In the midst of the applause that greets Rous's outburst, Roberts steps on to the platform. After a moment's silence some of the men try to prevent him from speaking but he quells the uproar with his eyes. Roberts's message is to fight, to fight against Nature and Capital. In a passionate and powerful speech, he harangues the men and demands that they fight for future generations of workers so that the capitalist class will no longer be able to treat the workers as dogs. Just as the approving shout for Roberts is being taken up by the men, Madge Thomas brings the news that Annie is dying. Total silence falls as Roberts leaps down from the platform, torn from his moment of triumph. Once he has gone Madge reveals that Annie is in fact dead. She hurls the question at the cowed men: 'How many more women are you going to let die?'

Nevertheless, many still want to stick by Roberts. At this point, Rous exploits the situation, turning the majority in favour of compromise. The cheers which now greet the idea of making terms with the Union are interrupted by Evans's accusation: 'Ye blacklegs!' Thomas steps in to stop the ensuing fight between Evans and Bulgin as the curtain falls.

Act III

In the Underwoods' artistically furnished drawing-room, Enid, who is sewing a baby's frock, tells Edgar, her brother, about her visit to Roberts's cottage. Her experience there has led to a change in her sympathies which are no longer totally with the strikers and their families. She still hopes that her father will make concessions but Edgar realises that because he will not the Board are likely to vote against him. Enid's feelings are now those of an affectionate daughter worried for her ageing father's health. Edgar, although obviously fond of his father, tries to maintain his stand of sympathy with the men. Under pressure from his sister he promises to do what he can to help his father and goes in to the dining-room where the other Directors have gathered. At the same moment Anthony appears through the other door on his way to the meeting. Enid tries to warn her father that he will be outvoted, but the old man refuses her plea not to attend the meeting.

In an attempt to do something constructive, Enid instructs Frost to show the men into the drawing-room when they arrive instead of leaving them in the cold hall. Frost chooses this moment to confide his own worries about his master's health. Anthony's obstinacy is underlined in Frost's comments about him. The butler has observed that the whole thing has become a struggle between Anthony and Roberts, whose personal grievance concerning poor financial reward for an invention that produced great profits for the Company is discounted by Frost. Impatient with his comments, Enid sends Frost to see if the Board members require tea.

The brief snatch of discussion heard as the doors open reveals that agreement is no nearer. As Frost returns, a parlourmaid enters to announce Madge Thomas, who brings the news of Annie's death, accusing Enid and Anthony of causing it. She underlines her statement that the poor get their own back on those who hurt them by making as if to threaten Enid's child by the look she casts on the baby's frock. Madge goes leaving Enid distressed, clutching the child's dress.

The doors open and Anthony walks across to an armchair into which he sinks slowly. Flushed, he does not respond to his daughter's enquiry, but Edgar, who has followed his father, reveals that Wilder has said Anthony is too old and feeble to know what he is doing. Immediately the other Directors flood into the room with Wilder making his apologies. They settle down in the drawing-room to continue their discussion, which reaches deadlock when Anthony still refuses to follow the opinion of the majority.

Edgar, who has been drawn outside by Enid, re-enters to break the news of Annie Roberts' death which he regards as the Directors' responsibility. He forcefully pursues his point about the suffering caused to the women and children, culminating in a decision to resign from the Board rather than continue to starve people. While Anthony stares at his son, the other Directors protest against his accusation, concerned lest any blame should be laid at their door by a Coroner's jury at the inquest into Annie's death. In a final attempt to reach agreement, Wilder proposes an amendment to the effect that the dispute should be placed in the hands of Simon Harness for settlement, on the lines indicated that morning. Before asking the Board to vote, Anthony finally states his position in full. It amounts to a decision to fight the class struggle, masters against men, in order to maintain the status quo and avoid 'mob government'.

Frost announces that the men have arrived but is told to keep them waiting; the Board must reach its decision. Matters come to a head between Anthony and his son, Edgar quietly pointing out that Mercy must be shown and his father admitting that he cannot understand the viewpoint of the younger generation. Anthony gives one final warning that to back down once in the face of such demands will lead to repeated confrontations in the future but his vote is the only one against Wilder's amendment. Anthony resigns from the Board and the men are brought in.

Roberts is missing from the delegation because of his wife's death. Harness arrives carrying the paper listing the men's demands. He joins Tench who has the Board's decision in writing. Unexpectedly Roberts does arrive, to tell the Board that the men will not compromise and that the Directors should return to London. Tench and Harness, however, have agreed terms which the Directors proceed to sign. The demands are conceded with the exception of those relating to the engineers and furnace men. The strike is at an end.

Roberts reads the paper and rounds on the men who, terrified of him, all protest. Harness comes to their aid by dismissing them. The Directors, with the exception of Edgar and Anthony, also rush off. Realising that Anthony has resigned, Roberts is first furiously emotional and then suddenly calm as he realises that both he and Anthony have been defeated. Harness tries to persuade Roberts to go home while Enid hurries in to look after her father.

As Anthony rises, he and Roberts gaze fixedly at each other, respect for his enemy dawning in each man's eyes. On his way out assisted by his two children, Anthony almost collapses. Roberts exits silently.

Tench and Harness, the two negotiators, remain. Where Tench is visibly quavering, Harness is pale and resolute. For Harness the settlement has entailed the death of a woman and the breaking of the two 'best' men. As Underwood, the Manager, enters, Tench excitedly comes to the realisation that the terms that have been agreed are the very same as those which were drawn up before the conflict began. He wants to know what it has all been for, a query which the enigmatic Harness answers: 'That's where the fun comes in!' As Underwood gestures his assent to this assertion, the curtain falls.

Commentary

Galsworthy and the theatre of his time

In 1906 when Galsworthy's first play, *The Silver Box,* was
produced at the Court Theatre, the staple diet of the majority of
London theatres still consisted of essentially lightweight, amusing
but trivial comedies, normally set in an upper-class drawing room.
Melodrama had lost its place as the most popular theatrical form
but the theatre was not a place for the expression of serious
thought. The style of acting and presentation was dominated by a
small group of Actor Managers, following in the footsteps of Sir
Henry Irving but lacking his talent and charismatic personality.
Productions were lavish, picturesque and romantic, each play a
suitable vehicle for its particular star.

The Bancrofts, a husband and wife partnership, working in close
collaboration with the dramatist Tom Robertson at the Prince of
Wales and Haymarket Theatres from the 1860s to the 1880s, had
begun to emphasise verisimilitude in setting and properties in their
productions of what were known as 'cup and saucer' plays. This
more 'natural' approach was extended in the work of the Actor
Manager John Hare (1844—1921) particularly in productions of
plays by Pinero at the St. James's Theatre. As the acting styles
became both more disciplined and more realistic, problems of
morality and class were dealt with in what can be called 'society
dramas', although the degree of social consciousness represented
in the plays of, for example, Henry Arthur Jones, Pinero and
Wilde, remains less than rigorously penetrating. Issues are raised
but rarely examined in depth and the outcome is determined by
theatrical conventions such as the desire, in the form of a 'happy'
ending, to re-establish the status quo and pretend that all will be
well rather than attempt to question the fundamental basis of what
is accepted as 'real life'. Although the revolution in the theatre on
the Continent was slow to reach England, the ground had been
prepared and change was inevitable.

In 1891 J.T. Grein (1862—1935) founded the Independent
Theatre, which was the equivalent of the so-called 'Free' theatres
on the Continent established to cater for serious, minority

audiences and to present the work of writers such as Ibsen,
Strindberg and Chekhov. Grein was responsible for the first British
production of Ibsen's *Ghosts* and it was greeted with much
controversy. To George Bernard Shaw, at this time a reviewer who
had not yet established himself as a playwright, Ibsen's work
represented a marvellously successful embodiment of what was to
be called the Theatre of Ideas. Whereas the critic Clement Scott,
scandalized by the subject matter, castigated the play as '. . . dull
undramatic uninteresting verbosity — formless, objectless,
pointless', Galsworthy supported Shaw in wishing to encourage
more playwrights to adopt Ibsen's serious approach to real life
issues. Their desire was to change the nature of what was presented
on the stage so that instead of being a place of mere entertainment,
the theatre would become '. . . a platform for discussion, for the
ventilation of new ideas'. They expected the playgoer 'to bring
mind and intelligence into the theatre' (A.E. Wilson, *Edwardian
Theatre*, p. 19) for the role of the playwright was to make his
audience *think*. Consequently they were determined to get rid
of what Shaw dubbed 'Sardoodledum', after the French playwright
Sardou, who relied heavily on mechanically complex plots to carry
his plays.

It must be remembered, however, that for many years, and in
some respects even today (if what is currently on offer in the bulk
of London's West End Theatres is anything to go by) this approach
to drama remained a minority viewpoint. The majority of
playgoers chose, and still choose, to attend theatres offering
entertainment above all. Thus Galsworthy's plays, with only one or
two exceptions (such as *Escape,* which ran for a year at the
Ambassadors Theatre), were often critical successes but financial
disasters. There was no public subsidy of the theatre. The money
to put on the plays was usually donated by a few wealthy
entrepreneurs, the best-known being Miss Annie Horniman, whose
private enthusiasm and personal funds brought into being the
Abbey Theatre in Dublin, the Gaiety, Manchester, and a season of
new plays at the Avenue Theatre, London.

By far the most outstanding director to emerge in England and
to choose this new breed of play as a vehicle was Harley
Granville Barker. Part of the legacy of the Bancrofts and Robertson
had been a more serious approach to the physical staging of the
plays and the rise in the significance of the stage director. Thus
when J.H. Leigh, a wealthy amateur actor, took on the lease of the
Court Theatre, he engaged both a manager — J.E. Vedrenne — and a

director — Granville Barker. Barker agreed to direct *The Two Gentlemen of Verona* in return for being able to give six matinées of *Candida* by G.B. Shaw. The experiment paid off and its success led to the period of the Vedrenne-Barker management of the Court from 18 October 1904 to 29 June 1907. The financial backing still came from Leigh but all artistic matters were in Barker's hands. The bulk of the plays he chose were by Shaw but he also presented Ibsen, translations of Euripides and comedies by St. John Hankin, as well as Galsworthy's first play, *The Silver Box*.

Galsworthy's interest in the theatre now became practical. He supervised casting and attended virtually all rehearsals, giving help and advice whenever he could. He admired Barker's work and obviously enjoyed being involved. He had decided views on acting style, which shed light on his approach to characterization. Actors were expected to sublimate their own personalities in order to create a convincing character on stage. To Dame Sybil Thorndike's cry, 'I can't do it. It's too hard. Do you want me to take away everything that is me?' Galsworthy replied, 'Yes. If you would do that, I think it would be quite all right.' (Short, *Sixty Years of Theatre*, p.120). Sharing the beliefs and attitudes of the new Theatre of Ideas, Galsworthy wrote his plays at the best possible moment for their accurate and successful interpretation.

Characters

John Anthony

At seventy six years of age and despite his white hair and occasionally faltering speech, Anthony retains all the powers of argument and force of character which have so far ensured that his will dominates the decisions of the Board of Directors. However, in the face of a potentially catastrophic fall in income if his policy of confrontation is pursued, the other Directors feel, for the first time, strong enough to vote against him.

Anthony's dynamism rests in his clear view of the world as a battleground between the classes to discover who should be master. His attitude towards his employees is that of the Old School where 'Masters are masters men are men!' (p.51). As far as he is concerned any suggestion that the workers are '. . . as good men as you' is 'Cant!' (p.9). He is consciously and deliberately fighting the men in order that his class may maintain its culture, its comforts, its superior position. Dismissing the pleas for compromise as nothing but sentiment and softness, he defines the role of the

Board as being 'to lead and to determine what is to be done and to do it without fear or favour' (p.51), for 'Give way to the men once and there'll be no end to it' (p.6). When his daughter pleads with him to agree to a compromise on the basis of her superior knowledge of the particular circumstances, he tries to make her see what would be the eventual and inevitable result:

> It's you who don't know the simple facts of the position. What sort of mercy do you suppose you'd get if no one stood between you and the continued demands of labour? This sort of mercy — [*he puts his hand up to his throat and squeezes it.*] First would go your sentiments, my dear; then your culture, and your comforts would be going all the time! (p.15)

Therefore to oppose what he sees as a revolutionary process, Anthony will fight in his own way to safeguard the future of his country which he sees 'threatened with mob government' (p.50). To give in, to compromise, would be to betray his country and class, to fail in his duty to Capital and make him 'ashamed to look my fellows in the face' (p.51). Edgar rightly describes his father's refusal to make concessions as 'a sort of religion with him' (p.40), for the principle of class supremacy is the bedrock of his father's personality. Any attempts to make him stand down because of his own failing health could never succeed since, in his eyes, his individual survival is not the most important matter to consider.

Anthony's strength of personality is underlined by the Board's inability to disagree with him in his presence (p.9). They complain behind his back but feel pushed to the brink of disaster before they have the courage to oppose him openly. He is, in fact, not a cruel man in personal terms. He has no desire to see women and children suffer, instructing Enid to give Annie Roberts 'what she wants, poor woman!' (p.15), but his paternalism does not contradict his pledge to maintain the superiority of his class — it is an intrinsic element in his philosophy.

At the end of the play, Anthony's silence and physical weakness embody his rejection; his decline represents the breaking down of the class barriers he has fought so hard to maintain. The middle men, the compromisers, have won, and his class has lost the battle.

Wilder, Wanklin and Scantlebury
Described as 'lean, cadaverous and complaining' (p.1), **Wilder's** overriding concern is money. Consequently he would like to oppose the Chairman but initially lacks the courage to do so. It is

only as his fears of losing money and being seen to be a poor businessman surface in Act 3 that he can force himself to stand up against Anthony and then his method is that of the petty insult (p.46). Careful of his own comforts as, for example, when he (symbolically) calls for a screen to protect himself from the heat of the fire (p.1), and worried about his own wife's health (p.47), he is totally without the imaginative response which would lead him to be concerned about the health of the strikers' wives and children. In fact, he takes comfort from the fact that the men will obviously be in a worse position than the Directors if the strike continues (p.5).

Wilder's admiration is reserved for the violent conduct of the employing class such as his own father, who shot one of his workers in the legs (p.3). His opportunism is demonstrated in his eagerness to get Harness to deal with the men since there could be problems (p.50, 53), whereas earlier (p.3) he had expressed severe reservations about Harness' trustworthiness.

Essentially selfish and mean, Wilder provides an obvious contrast with the courage and charisma of both Roberts and Anthony, a contrast which continues in the presentation of Wanklin and Scantlebury, both of whom also wish for a compromise settlement, mainly on account of the money that would be lost if the strike continued. The differences between these three and the Anthonys, both father and son, rest largely on the trio's inability to see beyond the cash nexus.

Wanklin, a more urbane figure than Wilder, fails to understand the real situation. He states: 'We needn't consider the Union' (p.4), but his pragmatic approach renders Anthony's principles meaningless when 'shares are below par' (p.6). His simplistic estimation of all events leads him to only one conclusion — compromise to reap the highest profits:

> Our only business is to see the Company earns as much profit as it safely can (p.47).

He lacks any ability to comprehend what either Anthony or Roberts is talking about; as far as he is concerned there is no problem.

Scantlebury, however, at least shows that he has feelings. At the suggestion that the Board are responsible for Annie Roberts' death, he screams almost hysterically that he is 'humane' (p.47). This 'very large, pale, sleepy man' (p.1) has shown from the outset a concern for his own physical comfort and some sympathy for the

condition of the men, 'Poor devils!' (p.1). However, his focus
throughout is upon food and warmth, neither of which the strikers
possess and the lack of which Scantlebury's tendency towards
sentimentalism can only ineffectually underline. When the
compromise is finally reached, he scuttles out after Wilder as if
terrified to remain with Roberts and Anthony. He tries to salve his
conscience by putting his name down for twenty pounds, if a fund
is started for the women and children, but remains the
embodiment of fear — fear of being too hot, too cold, of not
having enough good food but, above all, fear of men of principle
and courage bringing confrontation and discomfort in their wake.

Edgar and Enid Anthony

The Chairman's children do not share his principles. They are the
new generation caught between the die-hard elitism of their father
and the dynamic for social and industrial change expressed in the
men's decision to strike. Although their impulse is also towards
compromise, they are not weak-willed and their desire to improve
the lot of the men renders them attractive.

Edgar's very first statement hints at his sympathy with the men,
a sympathy which steadily grows. Initially he 'rather ashamedly'
suggests 'I think we ought to consider the men' (p.5), since he can
only see it as cruelty to push things so far in the face of all the
suffering involved. The death of Annie Roberts, following upon
hours of abortive discussion with Board members who steadfastly
refuse to consider anything other than the size of their dividends,
finally impels him towards resignation. He knows only too well
that the Directors do not mean to be cruel, but they lack the
imaginative power to be able to perceive the reality of the men's
situation and the true results of their own actions (p.49). Edgar
represents a moral stance, an attitude of conscious responsibility
towards the employees. He cannot accept that the profit motive
should dominate men's behaviour: 'Men of business are excused
from decency, you think?' (p.6).

From the scenes between the brother and sister, their sincere
affection for each other and their father is obvious. The difference
between them is that, where Enid finally puts her family's welfare
before that of the strikers, Edgar struggles against her arguments in
support of their father. Enid's sympathies are shown to be
essentially personal — as Edgar says: 'Your family or yourself and
over goes the show!' Her decision that their first duty is to save
their father is based on her narrow personal perspective, reinforced

by the dismissive treatment she has received at the hands of
Roberts. She is the archetypical middle-class 'do-gooder'. She hates
to see women and children suffer, particularly if she has personal
contact with them, as in the case of Annie, but as her father rightly
says, she does not see the whole reality of the situation. She has no
concept of the larger issues involved and in this sense does not
understand her father at all. She quite simply does not want
anybody to get hurt.

Edgar too, while wishing to remain true to his convictions that
the men should be treated decently, lacks the ability to apprehend
the scale of his father's thoughts. Unlike his father, he sees the
issue at Trenartha Tin Plate Works as one industrial dispute which
should be settled kindly; he has no appreciation of the nature of
class struggle as described by Anthony. It is this failure of
perception that leads their father to dismiss both of his children as
members of a 'soft breed' (p.52).

Harness and Underwood

Rather dismissive of the Board members' attention to their own
creature comforts and sympathetic to the poor living conditions of
the men, Francis Underwood gives the impression of being an
efficient Manager, who understands the men's position with regard
to the Union (p.4), in contrast to the ignorance of some of the
Directors. He also knows the strikers' strength of purpose (p.5).
Although married to the Chairman's daughter, he is treated very
much as an inferior, showing people in and out at the behest of
the Board (p.9). Despite his superior knowledge of local conditions,
he is ignored during discussion of the issues, unless information on
particular points is requested. Despite his greater affluence, he too
is an employee who, judging by his emotional response to Roberts'
accusation that he is an agent of his oppressive employers (p.12),
finds his position between the forces of Capital and Labour
difficult to endure.

Simon Harness, the Union official sent to resolve the problem of
strikers' demands which are out of line with Union policy, seems to
Wilder 'one of those cold-blooded, cool-headed chaps' (p.3), drawn
in deliberate contrast to Roberts, the 'fanatical firebrand'. Yet
Harness shares Roberts' bitterness that the men should be expected
to accept the bare essentials of life, whereas for the Directors
'. . . motor-cars, and champagne and eight-course dinners' (p.8) are
deemed essential. Harness' icy tone when dismissing Edgar's pity,
allied to his belief that all men are as good as each other, reveals a

determination that justice should be done. His method of coping
with Roberts' rather provocative attitude is to maintain a tone of
quiet reasonableness whilst trying to force Roberts to state his case
instead of merely insult the Directors. Where Roberts is a fighter,
Harness is a negotiator, to whom respect for the other side is vital
(p.11). He observes the first confrontation between Roberts and
Anthony with a 'faint smile' (p.12), an amusement that turns to a
far more serious understanding of the conflict he has witnessed. At
the end of the play, he remarks, '[*In a slow grim voice*] That's
where the fun comes in!' (p.56)

When he addresses the strikers, Harness explains that some of
their demands must be reduced in the name of justice to all. With
'cold passion' (p.30) he makes the case for unity, for, as he sees it:

> . . . the whole is greater than the part and you are only the part.
> Stand by us, and we will stand by you. (p.31)

Having dealt efficiently with suggestions that the Union may be
lying, he leaves the men to make up their own minds.

When he re-appears (p.53), he is carrying the paper signifying
the men's decision to negotiate through the Union. Although
Roberts ignores him, Harness manages at the third attempt to force
him to listen to the new statement of demands which, having been
acceded to by the Directors with the exception of Anthony, will
mean a return to work. Now he has their decision, Harness, whose
very name acquires significance, takes control and dismisses the
rest of the delegation as Roberts continues to rage. 'Pale and
resolute' (p.56), Harness remains in possession of the stage as the
curtain falls. The Old Order has been defeated, the new mode of
negotiation and compromise will now run its course.

David Roberts

Diametrically opposed to Anthony is Roberts whom we first meet
as the leader of the strikers' delegation. At this point he is the
dominant representative of the men's views, demonstrating an
almost hypnotic power over the others even when they apparently
disagree with him (p.10). Described by Wilder before he appears as
'a fanatical firebrand' (p.4), his manner of address recalls Hellfire
preaching. His fluent speech with its Biblical and 'Chapel'
overtones shows a conscious use of words even if only to goad and
insult his enemies (p.10).

His innate awareness of his own worth and dignity as a man is
rejected by his opponents: 'I mustn't speak my mind to the

Chairman but the Chairman may speak his mind to me!' (p.14). His passionate resentment of this attitude of superiority is reinforced by his feelings of having been exploited by the Company. For his invention, which he is sure earned the Company a hundred thousand pounds, he was paid only seven hundred. The impression, however, is never that of someone who is primarily concerned with money or material comforts. These are only necessary as methods by which a man may feel himself properly valued as a human being. It is the inhumanity of a system based on Capital which Roberts is up in arms against. As his wife bears witness,

> All of Roberts' savin's have gone. He's always looked forward to this strike. He says he's no right to a farthing when the others are suffering. (p.24).

Just as Anthony will fight to safeguard the status quo so Roberts will fight to change it:

> 'Tis not for this little moment of time we're fighting, not for ourselves, our own little bodies and their wants, 'tis for all those that come after throughout all time. (p.37)

Both men know the scale of the struggle in which they are involved; it is this consciousness which separates them from the other characters whose only concerns are the immediate circumstances of the strike.

Roberts' rebuttal of Thomas' insistence that the men must surrender to Nature signifies his determination to shape his own destiny:

> 'Tis only by that − [*he strikes a blow with his clenched fist*] − in Nature's face that a man can be a man. (p.35)

His demagogic control of the reactions of the strikers in Act III through rhetoric and emotive language skilfully convinces the audience both of his ability to lead men and of his sincerity. He knows he is right and will not flinch from the violence that will be necessary to resolve the situation of Labour against Capital (p.35).

His whole consciousness, however, is so closely tied to the principle at stake that his personal relationship with his wife inevitably suffers. He calls her 'my girl' with great affection and wraps his coat around her but desperately avoids thinking too closely about her real condition. When she accuses him of not caring whether women die as a result of the struggle, he breaks off in mid-sentence, 'No one will die till we have beaten these −' and

cannot meet her eyes. He knows the truth but in this personal
context cannot accept it. Ironically, it is the death of his wife
which forces him to leave the strike meeting, enabling Madge and
Rous to turn the majority in favour of compromise.

Despite his wife's death, Roberts turns up unexpectedly to act
as part of the delegation, still determined to fight, not knowing
that the men have already given in. He insists: 'Ye made a mistake
to think that we would come to heel. Ye may break the body but
ye cannot break the spirit' (p.54), but this courageousness leads to
callousness in his attitude towards all, whether it be his arch enemy
— 'If I saw Mr. Anthony going to die and I could save him by
lifting my hand, I would not lift the little finger of it' (p.25) — or
the thoughtless majority of working people:

> MRS. ROBERTS. But think o' the children, David.
> ROBERTS. Ah! If they will go breeding themselves for slaves
>   without a thought o' the future o' them they breed — (p.26).

A man of principle who respects those who are equally strong
(p.25), Roberts lacks the more delicate feelings of human
sympathy for those weaker than himself.

The women

Act II Scene I opens on a 'clean, tidy, very barely furnished'
kitchen in Roberts' cottage. Seated around a meagre fire, five
women, whose families are all involved in the strike, are talking.
Through their conversation, the nature of their poverty- and
disaster-stricken lives is revealed. And yet, despite a diet of bread
and tea and the only warmth for the children being found by
keeping them in bed, the women exhibit a dogged if tremulous
cheerfulness. As Mrs. Rous says: 'We're all going the same way'
(p.20).

Annie Roberts, Enid Underwood's former maid and now the
wife of the strike leader, appears only in this one scene and yet her
shadow looms over the whole play as the symbol of the suffering
endured by the workers. In the company of the other women she is
quietly hospitable but assertive on the subject of her husband's
fight for what is right when Madge Thomas questions the nature of
his control over the men. Although Annie's disquiet at Enid's visit
is shown by her flinching when her former employer appears, she is
deferentially polite in direct contrast to the deliberate rudeness
displayed by Madge. Her courtesy, however, in no way denotes any
disloyalty to her husband. She quietly refutes all of Enid's

attempts to persuade her to agree that the strike — and Roberts — are wrong. Her husband's name is frequently cited as a source of authority; Annie believes passionately in his view of the working man's lot to the extent that she has been willing to forgo the pleasure of bearing children since '. . . without a man is very near and pinches and stints 'imself and 'is children to save, there can't be neither surplus nor security' (p.24). To bring children into a world of such hardship is irresponsible and wrong.

Annie knows her husband's 'wild' nature and in private will try to make him realise how the women are thinking. There is the occasional flash of malice when she comes up against his stubbornness but almost immediately this is superseded by a soft, gentle request that he should take back his overcoat to protect himself from the cold. There is bitterness in the knowledge that her husband feels it is more important to attend the strike meeting than to stay to look after her.

Her courage in bearing extreme pain underlines the strength and determination of this dying woman. Her excitement at the sounds of the strikers' meeting demonstrates her total commitment to her husband's view of the future. Her pain and pleasure symbolise the experience and anticipation of change felt by the strikers.

Madge Thomas, 'a good-looking girl of twenty-two', does not accept that it is necessary to suffer such deprivation for the sake of future benefits. She relates to Annie the stand she has adopted towards her lover, George Rous. In the manner of Lysistrata in the comedy by Aristophanes, where the women refuse to have sex with their husbands until they make peace, Madge uses her own sexuality as a bargaining counter: 'If Rous wants me he must give up Roberts' (p.20). The ferocity of her temper manifests itself when Enid appears. In the face of this common enemy, whom she accuses of being a 'spy', Madge refuses to acknowledge that there is any suffering. The antagonism between the vibrant working girl and the sensitive Chairman's daughter continues when Madge takes Annie's final dying request to Enid. The savagery in Madge comes to the fore as she accuses Enid, 'for all your soft words' (p.45), of being as responsible as anyone else for Annie's death. She instinctively knows the essentially ineffectual nature of Enid's sympathy. To frighten Enid, she symbolically threatens the life of her baby by her sudden swift movement and fixed stare at the child's frock. (p.45)

Within the immediate context, Madge is partially responsible for Roberts' defeat. It is her emotional blackmailing of Rous that leads

the young man to step in to manipulate the strikers after Roberts
has left to go to Annie. Madge dramatically prepares the way for
talk of compromise by hurling her challenge at the confused men:
'You pack of blinded hounds! How many more women are you
going to let die?'

The 'spitfire' (p.38) is grudgingly admired; her energy and
passion have their effect on men whose spirits have been weakened
by the long drawn-out struggle. She is the enemy within.

The men

Although none of the other strikers are depicted in the same detail
as Roberts, several are afforded individuality by their appearance
and differences of opinion as to the future of the strike. Henry
Thomas and George Rous are the most significant of these.

In his speech and attitudes, **Thomas** is a born son of the Welsh
Chapel. Religious teaching has led him to believe that humble
submissiveness to what is ordained by Nature should be the men's
response. He tries to stand out against Roberts in Act I but is
defeated by the latter's sarcasm and powerful personality. This
does not defeat him permanently, however, for he arrives at
Roberts' cottage just before the meeting in the hope of persuading
him to change his opinion. Unlike his daughter, he respects Roberts
for his integrity as well as his courage (p.28). At the strike meeting
he makes his plea to the men:

> This Nature must pe humort. It is a man's pisiness to pe pure,
> honest, just and merciful. That's what Chapel tells you. And,
> look you, David Roberts, Chapel tells you ye can do that
> without coing against Nature. (p.32)

As far as he is concerned 'We haf fought fair and if we haf peen
beaten, it iss no fault of ours', but he has no faith in a Union that
has done nothing to improve his working conditions for the twenty
five years he has been a member. He believes the strike is an
isolated occurrence which should be settled by the men and the
Board.

George Rous, on the other hand, eventually argues for the
intervention of the Union to achieve a compromise settlement.
Rous, in fact, is initially a staunch supporter of Roberts — even just
before the meeting, Thomas tells Annie Roberts that her husband's
only support lies with 'the engineers and George Rous' (p.28) —
but Rous has his mind changed for him by the blackmailing antics
of the girl he loves. If he wishes to marry Madge, he must renege on

Roberts; her ultimatum is stark and she knows it will succeed. Hence Rous' air of 'fierce distraction' (p.34) and the excited manner in which he addresses the men. His advice now is:

> Chuck it up! Chuck it up! Sooner than go on starving the women and the children. (p.34)

When Roberts leaves the meeting, it is Rous, the young man who 'looks like a soldier' with 'a glitter in his eyes' (p.10), who turns the tide in favour of compromise.

Why not 'Strike'?

To read many reactions both of audience and critics to *Strife* is to receive the impression that Galsworthy's intention and achievement was to dramatise the issues of a particular strike. Certainly in terms of his intentions nothing could be further from the truth as may be seen from his letter of October 1931 to William Armstrong, the Director of the Liverpool Repertory Theatre:

> . . . the strike, which forms the staple material of the play, was only chosen by me as a convenient vehicle to carry the play's real theme, which is that of the Greek 'hubris' or violence; *Strife* is, indeed, a play on extremism or fanaticism.

The title chosen is thus apposite since it draws attention deliberately to the real intention of the playwright. However, whether he actually manages to show 'human nature in the thick of a fight, the "heroism" of die-hardism and the nemesis that dogs it' (with the particular struggle between Capital and Labour at the Trenartha Tin Plate Works serving merely as a convenient example of this) is more problematic. *Strife* may not be a 'photographic reproduction of an industrial struggle' but the very success of the characterisation of the two protagonists tends to ground the play in its immediate context, which is reinforced by a failure to extend the arguments they advance about Capital and Labour into a wider discussion of more universal significance. Thus *Strife* deals with only one type of fanaticism — that arising from the extreme antagonism between industrial workers and those who are determined to remain their masters. It is only through a fuller knowledge of Galsworthy's own attitudes and view of life that it becomes possible to see the play as something more than a plea for a constructive and optimistic appraisal of each man's role in this particular arena.

    Galsworthy frequently had to endure his plays' concerns and

impact being reduced to the level of immediate issues. The most celebrated instance was the reception accorded *Justice,* which was interpreted as a piece of special pleading for prisoners undergoing solitary confinement. It had the remarkable effect of achieving reform of the law but Galsworthy, although delighted, steadfastly insisted that his play was concerned with wider issues relating to the Nature of Man:

> Honestly, the public . . . so jolly well miss the main line of the play that one is more than ever discouraged from taking subjects which can be whittled down to one small issue by the practical — to the neglect of the fundamental criticism on human life . . . The public — bless them — take it for a tract on solitary confinement . . . (Letter to W.L. George)

Perhaps the answer to this recurring problem of 'wrong-headed' interpretation may lie, as Benedict Nightingale suggests, in Galsworthy's lack of cosmic vision (*50 Modern British Plays,* p.107). An audience senses there is no 'deeper perspective', that there are no 'larger questions about the fate of the society to which they belonged'. This is not, however, to denigrate what is achieved, merely to suggest that an audience can on occasions react more accurately to what is being presented than an author can determine in advance. Within its limits — a powerful depiction of one example of the effects of fanaticism — *Strife* is seen as a most successful play but one that is locked in the context of early twentieth-century English society and necessarily lacking the resonance of classic Greek tragedy for which Galsworthy was aiming.

Thus runs the accepted critical assessment of *Strife.* But it omits crucial consideration of Galsworthy's very individual style, which is not merely naturalistic. If it were so, it might be possible to accept a 'documentary' interpretation of his work, but, given Galsworthy's own pronouncements on the topic, it would be unwise not to look closer.

In his essay *Some Platitudes Concerning Drama,* written in the same year as *Strife,* Galsworthy clearly underlines his own understanding of the technique of naturalism as being only superficially life-like in a photographic sense and, in fact, being 'in every respect as dependent on imagination, construction, selection and elimination — the main laws of artistry — as ever was the romantic or rhapsodic play'. A keen playgoer himself, Galsworthy's dramatic theory contains many insights into, and much good sense about, theatrical practice. The man often considered to be the

arch-naturalist reveals an attitude towards realism contrary to
accepted belief; the true realist, in Galsworthy's eyes, occupied
himself with showing the way in which what he called 'the spirit of
life' was intermixed with thought and personality. His plea is for
the underlying truths of life to be expressed upon the stage:

> Let us have starlight, moonlight, sunlight and the light of our
> own self-respects.

Indeed Galsworthy's determination to avoid the photographic or
documentary approach of mainstream Naturalism is forcefully
expressed in the Introduction to the Manaton edition of his plays:

> It can be seen how a dramatist, strongly and pitifully impressed
> by the encircling pressure of modern environments, predisposed
> to the naturalistic method, and with something in him of the
> satirist, will neither create characters seven or even six feet high,
> nor write plays detached from the movements and problems of
> his times. He is not conscious, however, of any desire to solve
> those problems in his plays, or to effect dire reforms. His only
> ambition in drama, as in his other work, is to present truth as he
> sees it, and, gripping with it his readers or his audience, to
> produce in them a sort of mental and moral fermenting whereby
> vision may be enlarged, imagination livened, and understanding
> promoted.'

A glance at the structure of *Strife* reveals a deliberate patterning,
an architectural form that has been selected to present an impartial
balance of forces so that the worlds of Labour and Capital are
shown with equal clarity and fairness. The conflict between
Anthony and Roberts has the flavour of inevitability and, as can be
seen from the play's success in the 1970s both at the National
Theatre and on television, possesses a timelessness one would not
expect if it were nothing but the dramatisation of a particular
strike. The Greek quality of hubris, one of the causes of true
Tragedy identified by Aristotle, can be seen expressed in the pride,
arrogance and fanaticism of the two protagonists.

Unlike the conventional naturalist, Galsworthy uses irony, pity
and indignation to comment upon the folly of mankind. Roberts
and Anthony are representative types; we are not even told any
precise details of the strike or the men's demands for these are not
what is important in Galsworthy's view. He is not committed to
analysing the ills of a particular situation but illustrating a universal
dilemma. The two die-hards represent absolutes of strength and

power in the struggle with Nature — hence the importance of
Thomas' intervention arguing for the domination of Man by Nature
(p.32). Roberts and Anthony, linked as brothers-in-defeat as they
finally mutually acknowledge each other's qualities, symbolise the
failure of modern English society actively to shape its own future.
The negative force of compromise is victorious instead.

Much is made of Galsworthy's legal training and impulse
towards a balanced view. The critic, James Agate, made fun of his
celebrated humanity:

> The writer is in himself an entire Humane Society. He sides with
> the fox against the man in pink, the hen-coop against the
> marauding fox, the chickweed against the chicken, and whatever
> it is the chickweed preys on against the ferocious plant.

But this is not the final impression of Galsworthy that we are left
with at the end of *Strife*. The theatrical impact of Roberts and
Anthony is designed to be on a heroic scale. Those who oppose
them from within their own camps seem weak, vacillating,
unimaginative or selfish by comparison. Within the Absolute Law
to which these leaders owe their allegiance, individual deaths are of
no significance for what matters is the outcome of the battle. We
are led to consider the true nature of such a compromise as takes
place. Galsworthy noted in his letter to W. Armstrong, that
Anthony and Roberts 'are certainly the only characters in the play
who can be called heroic . . . they are also by reason of their
extremism the villains of the piece'. However, Galsworthy's skill
in exposing the unattractive weaknesses of the other characters
leads an audience to dismiss any alternative offered by them. No
matter what the playwright may claim, in terms of their emotional
impact on an audience and the identification an audience feels with
them, it is the extremists who emerge the apparent victors.

Galsworthy as a dramatist

Although it took Galsworthy almost a decade of painstaking
application to achieve recognition as a novelist, his theatrical career
began with an overnight success. The production of *The Silver Box*
at the Court Theatre by the Vedrenne-Barker management in 1906
led Galsworthy's name to be linked with George Bernard Shaw's as
dramatists of the new Theatre of Ideas. Performances of *Strife* in
1909 confirmed and extended his reputation.

Galsworthy's dramatic method as exemplified by *Strife* demonstrates, in William Archer's words:

> a classic ease of composition and draughtmanship. The structure is good, the characterisation clear and animated; there is nothing freakish, nothing excessive . . .

It is a method which relies upon a series of contrasts, contrasts of character and setting reinforced by a deliberate balancing of opposites.

The play opens in the well-appointed comfort of the manager's house, moves to the meagre abode of Roberts, to the barren space where the strike meeting takes place and then back to what now seems, by comparison, a luxurious setting. Thus the audience receives a powerful visual impression of the material differences between the workers and the employers. The contrast is heightened by such touches as Scantlebury's compalint about too much heat from the fire in the manager's dining-room compared to the total absence of warmth experienced by Annie Roberts. He thinks he will expire from too much heat, she dies from lack of it.

The action of the play takes place between noon and the evening of one day. This condensing of the timescale creates a taut framework and heightens the tension, lending an aura of inevitability to the battle in which the alternative versions of fanaticism are routed at the last gasp by a final failure of nerve in the supporters of each charismatic leader.

George Bernard Shaw himself drew attention to the major difference between his own dramatic method and that of Galsworthy. He contrasted his 'downright barnstorming' with 'the subtler ways of . . . Mr. Galsworthy' (Letter to the editor of the *Saturday Review*, 2 July 1910). This subtlety has been defined recently by G. Lloyd Evans as 'a kind of stealth of technique, a quiet deviousness in characterization and, above all, a quality of associativeness in the language' (*The Language of Modern Drama*, p.65). Galsworthy himself in the essay *Some Platitudes Concerning Drama* distinguished three types of dramatist, the third of which he clearly perceived as matching his own approach:

> To set before the public no cut-and-dried codes but the phenomena of life and character, selected and combined but not distorted, by the dramatist's outlook, set down without fear, favour or prejudice, leaving the public to draw such poor moral as nature may afford.

Whereas with Shaw the reader is always aware of exactly what response is expected by the author, the signalling process used by Galsworthy is indeed far more subtle. Apart from very brief physical descriptions of each character, as in the opening stage direction delineating each member of the Board, it seems at first glance that we have to find our own way through the dialogue; after all in Galsworthy's eyes character is established through action and dialogue, not by authorial intervention. Certainly our impressions of Anthony, the immovable object, and Roberts, the irresistible force, are founded in the detailed statements of their own point of view. In this sense Galsworthy's legal training does appear to have paid dividends in that he proves an exceptionally powerful writer of what are often called 'set speeches'. However, if we believe that here is nothing other than the presentation of a balanced view which allows each member of the audience to decide who is right, then we ignore the touches of 'deviousness in characterization' which Galsworthy includes as directions to actor and director and, finally, to the audience.

Galsworthy's stage directions may be relatively small in number and length but they are nevertheless vitally important. Each character's appearance is deftly outlined with physical characteristics often giving the key to basic personality traits, thus Bulgin has a 'fighting jaw' (p.9) and Enid 'a small, decided face' (p.2). Without the descriptions within the stage directions at the opening of Act II Scene I, the deliberately contrasting types Galsworthy envisaged within the small group of strikers' wives would be far more difficult for actresses to create.

It is also within the stage directions that the theme of 'ways of seeing' is most clearly embodied. Virtually every character's eyes are described according to their ability to perceive reality. John Anthony's 'movements are rather slow and feeble but his eyes are very much alive' and Underwood's eyes are 'steady'. Roberts is given 'small fiery eyes', Green's are 'mild, straightforward' and Rous' eyes have 'a glitter' in them. That 'eyes are the window of the soul' would seem to be axiomatic to Galsworthy. Thus the power of a glance from Anthony can quell the Board members just as Roberts' long, steady stare brings the strike meeting to order. At the end of the play, these two gaze 'at each other fixedly' and, having found the truth of the quality and strength of each, finally 'bend their heads in token of respect'. But only they can take the force of each other's glance. The strikers can only vote against Roberts when he is absent and the Board members avert their eyes from their Chairman when voting. The feeling of waste at the end of the play owes much to the defeat of those with the power to see the truth (here equated with courage and zest for life) by those with a desire for easy living within a narrow perspective.

Galsworthy's skill in writing dialogue which delineates character is obvious even in relatively minor cases such as Scantlebury whose indecisiveness and insecurity comes across so positively and yet unobtrusively in the 'H'm's, Dear, dear's' and numerous repetitions which litter his utterances, preparing the way for the near hysteria which breaks from him when he feels accused of Annie Roberts' death (p.49). When the ritualistic biblical rhythm which is a source of strength in Roberts' words is adopted by others, it is interestingly exposed as a façade for men who wish to evade responsibility for their own destiny, as is the case with Thomas. Where Roberts *uses* the rhetoric of the Chapel, Thomas can only repeat the phrases − 'It is a man's pisiness to pe pure, honest, just and merciful' (p.32). This simplistic belief cannot compare with the rhetorical power of:

> If we have not the hearts of men to stand against it breast to breast, and eye to eye, and force it backward till it cry for mercy, it will go on sucking life; and we shall stay for ever what we are [*in almost a whisper*] less than the very dogs. (p.37)

Galsworthy weighs matters even further against Thomas by deliberately underlining the comic impact of the extreme Welshness (even 'stage Welshness') of this pronunciation in phonically representing peculiarities such as 'p's for 'b's and 't's for 'd's. The inclusion of the cliché expression 'look you', never used by any real Welshman, reinforces Galsworthy's intention to portray Thomas as little more than the sincere 'plucked chicken' suggested by the stage direction (p.10).

Traditional theatricality may seem dominant in *Strife* in terms of setting and characterization but there are elements quite unlike the usual mode of naturalism and more akin to symbolism present in the play. In Act II Scene I, the argument between Madge and Rous is constantly undercut by the young lad, Jan Thomas, playing his penny whistle. He imitates the call of the cuckoo. The potential of this counterpointing is clear to G. Lloyd Evans:

> It amounts to a wordless comment on man's stupidity; it is as if Feste or Lear's Fool, in the guise of a child, had entered and in their sad, objective way, punctuated the harsh reality of this

world with the timeless irony of 'but that's all one!'. (*The Language of Modern Drama*, p.78)

A further technique which both facilitates dramatic focus and gives the play an added dimension is the introduction of the two extraneous characters, the Bargemen, who observe the strike meeting. Initially they 'lounge and smoke indifferently' (p.30) on the towpath in the background. As the meeting proceeds in its bleak landscape, Galsworthy uses these two observers to comment upon the action. It is as if this particular battle is of active interest to the outside world. The presence of the Bargemen enlarges the significance of the events of the play. At one point they laugh at what is said; when Harness leaves, one of them jerks 'his pipe with a derisive gesture' (p.31). Tension and expectancy are heightened when one of the Bargemen rises to listen attentively to Roberts. That simple action momentarily dominates the stage, forcing the audience to focus all of its attention upon the speaker.

Such components have their linguistic counterpart in the treatment of 'heat'. The play opens with Wilder and Scantlebury frantically trying to escape from the heat of the dining-room fire, representing their desire to evade the full-blooded passions of reality embodied in the fire of the men's wrath. Christopher Morahan in his production at the National Theatre in 1978 made concrete this link by placing the indoor scene downstage whilst upstage raged the noise and hot glow from the Trenartha Works, recalling the fires of Hell. Where the strikers and their wives confront and endure the ravages of the elements, the majority of the Directors retreat from any contact with the reality represented by the elemental world. Where Anthony speaks of 'the black waters of confusion' and Roberts begs the men not to 'blacken the sky an' let the bitter sea in over them', the compromisers wish to reduce the context of the argument and hence man's potential. Absolutes such as heat and cold must be avoided or screened off — a symbolic counterpoint to the theme of moderation, which is also an attempt to mediate between absolutes of power.

Thus the language, visual and aural, of the play undercuts and informs that naturalism which is so often considered Galsworthy's greatest strength. It is largely this extension of the immediate into a universal apprehension of the nature and condition of man that renders *Strife* a play of continuing interest and Galsworthy a playwright whose accomplishment has yet to be fully appreciated.

Further reading

Galsworthy's Works
The Plays of John Galsworthy, Duckworth, 1929
Five Plays, Methuen, 1984
Candelabra (Essays including Some Platitudes Concerning Drama),
  Heinemann, 1932

Many of the novels including all parts of *The Forsyte Saga* and
A Modern Comedy are available in Penguin paperback editions.

Biographical
The Life and Letters of John Galsworthy: H.V. Marrot,
  Heinemann, 1935
Galsworthy the Man: Rudolf Sauter, Peter Owen, 1967
John Galsworthy: Catherine Dupré, Collins, 1976

Criticism
The Man of Principle: Dudley Barker, Heinemann, 1964
John Galsworthy: A Survey: Leon Schalit, Heinemann, 1929
Galsworthy's Plays: A Critical Survey: A.D. Choudhuri, Orient
  Longmans, Calcutta, 1961
The Language of Modern Drama: G. Lloyd Evans, Dent, 1977
An Introduction to 50 Modern British Plays: Benedict
  Nightingale, Pan, 1982

Theatrical Background
The Old Drama and the New: William Archer, Heinemann, 1923
Edwardian Theatre: A.E. Wilson, Arthur Barker, 1951
Sixty Years of Theatre: Ernest Short, Eyre & Spottiswoode, 1951
The Revels History of Drama in English Volume III (1880 to the
  present day) ed. Hunt, Richards and Russell, Methuen, 1978

STRIFE

A DRAMA IN THREE ACTS

ACT I.,   *The dining-room of the Manager's house.*

ACT II.,   SCENE I.   *The kitchen of the Roberts' cottage near the works.*

SCENE II.   *A space outside the works.*

ACT III.,   *The drawing-room of the Manager's house.*

The action takes place on February 7th between the hours of noon and six in the afternoon, close to the Trenartha Tin Plate Works, on the borders of England and Wales, where a strike has been in progress throughout the winter.

CAST OF THE ORIGINAL PRODUCTION
At the Duke of York's Theatre on March 9, 1909.

JOHN ANTHONY	*Mr. Norman McKinnel*
EDGAR ANTHONY	*Mr. C. M. Hallard*
FREDERIC WILDER	*Mr. Dennis Eadie*
WILLIAM SCANTLEBURY. . . .	*Mr. Luigi Lablache*
OLIVER WANKLIN	*Mr. Charles V. France*
HENRY TENCH	*Mr. O. P. Heggie*
FRANCIS UNDERWOOD	*Mr. A. S. Holmwood*
SIMON HARNESS	*Mr. George Ingleton*
DAVID ROBERTS	*Mr. J. Fisher White*
JAMES GREEN	*Mr. R. Luisk*
JOHN BULGIN	*Mr. P. L. Julian*
HENRY THOMAS	*Mr. H. R. Hignett*
GEORGE ROUS	*Mr. Owen Roughwood*
JAGO	*Mr. Charles Danvers*
EVANS.	*Mr. Drelincourt Odlam*
FROST	*Mr. Edward Gwenn*
ENID UNDERWOOD	*Miss Ellen O'Malley*
ANNIE ROBERTS	*Miss Mary Barton*
MADGE THOMAS	*Miss Lillah McCarthy*
MRS. ROUS	*Miss Rose Cazalet*
MRS. BULGIN	*Miss Sidney Paxton*
MRS. YEO	*Miss Blanche Stanley*

ACT I

*It is noon. In the Underwoods' dining-room a bright fire is burning. On
one side of the fireplace are double doors leading to the drawing-room,
on the other side a door leading to the hall. In the centre of the room
a long dining-table without a cloth is set out as a board table. At the
head of it, in the Chairman's seat, sits* JOHN ANTHONY, *an old man,
big, clean shaven, and high-coloured, with thick white hair, and thick
dark eyebrows. His movements are rather slow and feeble, but his
eyes are very much alive. There is a glass of water by his side. On
his right sits his son* EDGAR, *an earnest-looking man of thirty, reading
a newspaper. Next him* WANKLIN, *a man with jutting eyebrows,
and silver-streaked light hair, is bending over transfer papers.* TENCH,
*the secretary, a short and rather humble, nervous man, with side whiskers,
stands helping him. On* WANKLIN'S *right sits* UNDERWOOD, *the
Manager, a quiet man, with a long, stiff jaw, and steady eyes. Back
to the fire is* SCANTLEBURY, *a very large, pale, sleepy man, with grey
hair, rather bald. Between him and the Chairman are two empty
chairs.*

WILDER. [*Who is lean, cadaverous, and complaining, with drooping
grey moustaches, stands before the fire*] I say, this fire's the devil ! Can
I have a screen, Tench ?

SCANTLEBURY. A screen, ah !

TENCH. Certainly, Mr. Wilder. [*He looks at* UNDERWOOD.]
That is—perhaps the Manager—perhaps Mr. Underwood——

SCANTLEBURY. These fireplaces of yours, Underwood——

UNDERWOOD. [*Roused from studying some papers*] A screen ? Rather !
I'm sorry. [*He goes to the door with a little smile.*] We're not accus-
tomed to complaints of too much fire down here just now.

[*He speaks as though he holds a pipe between his teeth, slowly,
ironically.*]

WILDER. [*In an injured voice*] You mean the men. H'm !

[UNDERWOOD *goes out.*

SCANTLEBURY. Poor devils !

WILDER. It's their own fault, Scantlebury.

EDGAR. [*Holding out his paper*] There's great distress amongst
them, according to the *Trenartha News.*

WILDER. Oh, that rag ! Give it to Wanklin. Suit his Radical
views. They call us monsters, I suppose. The editor of that rubbish
ought to be shot.

1

EDGAR. [*Reading*] " If the Board of worthy gentlemen who control the Trenartha Tin Plate Works from their armchairs in London, would condescend to come and see for themselves the conditions prevailing amongst their workpeople during this strike——"

WILDER. Well, we *have* come.

EDGAR. [*Continuing*] " We cannot believe that even their leg-of-mutton hearts would remain untouched."

[WANKLIN *takes the paper from him.*

WILDER. Ruffian! I remember that fellow when he hadn't a penny to his name; little snivel of a chap that's made his way by blackguarding everybody who takes a different view to himself.

[ANTHONY *says something that is not heard.*

WILDER. What does your father say?

EDGAR. He says " The kettle and the pot."

WILDER. H'm! [*He sits down next to* SCANTLEBURY.

SCANTLEBURY. [*Blowing out his cheeks*] I shall boil if I don't get that screen.

[UNDERWOOD *and* ENID *enter with a screen, which they place before the fire.* ENID *is tall; she has a small, decided face, and is twenty-eight years old.*

ENID. Put it closer, Frank. Will that do, Mr. Wilder? It's the highest we've got.

WILDER. Thanks, capitally.

SCANTLEBURY. [*Turning, with a sigh of pleasure*] Ah! Merci, Madame!

ENID. Is there anything else you want, father? [ANTHONY *shakes his head.*] Edgar—anything?

EDGAR. You might give me a " J " nib, old girl.

ENID. There are some down there by Mr. Scantlebury.

SCANTLEBURY. [*Handing a little box of nibs*] Ah! your brother uses " J's." What does the manager use? [*With expansive politeness.*] What does your husband use, Mrs. Underwood?

UNDERWOOD. A quill!

SCANTLEBURY. The homely product of the goose.

[*He holds out quills.*

UNDERWOOD. [*Dryly*] Thanks, if you can spare me one. [*He takes a quill.*] What about lunch, Enid?

ENID. [*Stopping at the double doors and looking back*] We're going to have lunch here, in the drawing-room, so you needn't hurry with your meeting. [WANKLIN *and* WILDER *bow, and she goes out.*

SCANTLEBURY. [*Rousing himself, suddenly*] Ah! Lunch! That hotel—— Dreadful! Did you try the whitebait last night? Fried fat!

WILDER. Past twelve! Aren't you going to read the minutes, Tench?

TENCH. [*Looking for the* CHAIRMAN'S *assent, reads in a rapid and monotonous voice*] " At a Board Meeting held the 31st of January at the Company's Offices, 512, Cannon Street, E.C.   Present—Mr. Anthony in the chair, Messrs. F. H. Wilder, William Scantlebury, Oliver Wanklin, and Edgar Anthony.   Read letters from the Manager dated January 20th, 23rd, 25th, 28th, relative to the strike at the Company's Works.   Read letters to the Manager of January 21st, 24th, 26th, 29th.   Read letter from Mr. Simon Harness, of the Central Union, asking for an interview with the Board.   Read letter from the Men's Committee, signed David Roberts, James Green, John Bulgin, Henry Thomas, George Rous, desiring conference with the Board ; and it was resolved that a special Board Meeting be called for February 7th at the house of the Manager, for the purpose of discussing the situation with Mr. Simon Harness and the Men's Committee on the spot.   Passed twelve transfers, signed and sealed nine certificates and one balance certificate."

[*He pushes the book over to the* CHAIRMAN.

ANTHONY. [*With a heavy sigh*] If it's your pleasure, sign the same.

[*He signs, moving the pen with difficulty.*

WANKLIN. What's the Union's game, Tench ? They haven't made up their split with the men.   What does Harness want this interview for ?

TENCH. Hoping we shall come to a compromise, I think, sir ; he's having a meeting with the men this afternoon.

WILDER. Harness ! Ah ! He's one of those cold-blooded, cool-headed chaps. I distrust them. I don't know that we didn't make a mistake to come down. What time'll the men be here ?

UNDERWOOD. Any time now.

WILDER. Well, if we're not ready, they'll have to wait—won't do 'em any harm to cool their heels a bit.

SCANTLEBURY. [*Slowly*] Poor devils ! It's snowing. *What* weather !

UNDERWOOD. [*With meaning slowness*] This house'll be the warmest place they've been in this winter.

WILDER. Well, I hope we're going to settle this business in time for me to catch the 6.30. I've got to take my wife to Spain to-morrow. [*Chattily.*] My old father had a strike at his works in '69 ; just such a February as this.   They wanted to shoot him.

WANKLIN. What ! In the close season ?

WILDER. By George, there was no close season for employers then ! He used to go down to his office with a pistol in his pocket.

SCANTLEBURY. [*Faintly alarmed*] Not seriously ?

WILDER. [*With finality*] Ended in his shootin' one of 'em in the legs.

SCANTLEBURY. [*Unavoidably feeling his thigh*] No ?   God bless me !

ANTHONY. [*Lifting the agenda paper*] To consider the policy of the Board in relation to the strike.   [*There is a silence.*

WILDER. It's this infernal three-cornered duel—the Union, the men, and ourselves.

WANKLIN. We needn't consider the Union.

WILDER. It's my experience that you've always got to consider the Union, confound them ! If the Union were going to withdraw their support from the men, as they've done, why did they ever allow them to strike at all ?

EDGAR. We've had that over a dozen times.

WILDER. Well, I've never understood it ! It's beyond me. They talk of the engineers' and furnacemen's demands being excessive— so they are—but that's not enough to make the Union withdraw their support. What's behind it ?

UNDERWOOD. Fear of strikes at Harper's and Tinewell's.

WILDER. [*With triumph*] Afraid of other strikes—now, that's a reason ! Why couldn't we have been told that before ?

UNDERWOOD. You were.

TENCH. You were absent from the Board that day, sir.

SCANTLEBURY. The men must have seen they had no chance when the Union gave them up. It's madness.

UNDERWOOD. It's Roberts !

WILDER. Just our luck, the men finding a fanatical firebrand like Roberts for leader.   [*A pause.*

WANKLIN. [*Looking at* ANTHONY] Well ?

WILDER. [*Breaking in fussily*] It's a regular mess. I don't like the position we're in ; I don't like it ; I've said so for a long time. [*Looking at* WANKLIN.] When Wanklin and I came down here before Christmas it looked as if the men must collapse. You thought so too, Underwood.

UNDERWOOD. Yes.

WILDER. Well, they haven't ! Here we are, going from bad to worse—losing our customers—shares going down !

SCANTLEBURY. [*Shaking his head*] M'm ! M'm !

WANKLIN. What loss have we made by this strike, Tench ?

TENCH. Over fifty thousand, sir !

SCANTLEBURY. [*Pained*] You don't say !

WILDER. We shall never get it back.

TENCH. No, sir.

WILDER. Who'd have supposed the men were going to stick out like this—nobody suggested that.   [*Looking angrily at* TENCH.

SCANTLEBURY. [*Shaking his head*] I've never liked a fight—never shall.

ANTHONY. No surrender !   [*All look at him.*

WILDER. Who wants to surrender ?   [ANTHONY *looks at him.*] I—I want to act reasonably. When the men sent Roberts up to the Board in December—then was the time. We ought to have humoured him; instead of that, the Chairman—[*Dropping his eyes before* ANTHONY'S]—er—we snapped his head off. We could have got them in then by a little tact.

ANTHONY. No compromise!

WILDER. There we are! This strike's been going on now since October, and as far as I can see it may last another six months. Pretty mess we shall be in by then. The only comfort is, the men'll be in a worse!

EDGAR. [*To* UNDERWOOD] What sort of state are they really in, Frank?

UNDERWOOD. [*Without expression*] Damnable!

WILDER. Well, who on earth would have thought they'd have held on like this without support!

UNDERWOOD. Those who know them.

WILDER. I defy anyone to know them! And what about tin? Price going up daily. When we do get started we shall have to work off our contracts at the top of the market.

WANKLIN. What do you say to that, Chairman?

ANTHONY. Can't be helped!

WILDER. Shan't pay a dividend till goodness knows when!

SCANTLEBURY. [*With emphasis*] We ought to think of the share-holders. [*Turning heavily.*] Chairman, I say we ought to think of the shareholders.   [ANTHONY *mutters.*

SCANTLEBURY. What's that?

TENCH. The Chairman says he *is* thinking of you, sir.

SCANTLEBURY. [*Sinking back into torpor*] Cynic!

WILDER. It's past a joke. *I* don't want to go without a dividend for years if the Chairman does. We can't go on playing ducks and drakes with the Company's prosperity.

EDGAR. [*Rather ashamedly*] I think we ought to consider the men.

[*All but* ANTHONY *fidget in their seats.*

SCANTLEBURY. [*With a sigh*] We mustn't think of our private feelings, young man. That'll never do.

EDGAR. [*Ironically*] I'm not thinking of our feelings. I'm thinking of the men's.

WILDER. As to that—we're men of business.

WANKLIN. That *is* the little trouble.

EDGAR. There's no necessity for pushing things so far in the face of all this suffering—it's—it's cruel.

[*No one speaks, as though* EDGAR *had uncovered something whose existence no man prizing his self-respect could afford to recognize.*

WANKLIN. [*With an ironical smile*] I'm afraid we mustn't base our policy on luxuries like sentiment.

EDGAR. I detest this state of things.

ANTHONY. We didn't seek the quarrel.

EDGAR. I know that, sir, but surely we've gone far enough.

ANTHONY. No.   [*All look at one another*.

WANKLIN. Luxuries apart, Chairman, we must look out what we're doing.

ANTHONY. Give way to the men once and there'll be no end to it.

WANKLIN. I quite agree, but——   [ANTHONY *shakes his head*.] You make it a question of bedrock principle ?   [ANTHONY *nods*.] Luxuries again, Chairman !   The shares are below par.

WILDER. Yes, and they'll drop to a half when we pass the next dividend.

SCANTLEBURY. [*With alarm*] Come, come ! Not so bad as that.

WILDER. [*Grimly*] You'll see ! [*Craning forward to catch* ANTHONY'S *speech*.] I didn't catch——

TENCH. [*Hesitating*] The Chairman says, sir, " Fais que—que—devra——"

EDGAR. [*Sharply*] My father says : " Do what we ought—and let things rip."

WILDER. Tcha !

SCANTLEBURY. [*Throwing up his hands*] The Chairman's a Stoic—I always said the Chairman was a Stoic.

WILDER. Much good that'll do us.

WANKLIN. [*Suavely*] Seriously, Chairman, are you going to let the ship sink under you, for the sake of—a principle ?

ANTHONY. She won't sink.

SCANTLEBURY. [*With alarm*] Not while I'm on the Board I hope.

ANTHONY. [*With a twinkle*] Better rat, Scantlebury.

SCANTLEBURY. What a man !

ANTHONY. I've always fought them ; I've never been beaten yet.

WANKLIN. We're with you in theory, Chairman. But we're not all made of cast-iron.

ANTHONY. We've only to hold on.

WILDER. [*Rising and going to the fire*] And go to the devil as fast as we can !

ANTHONY. Better go to the devil than give in !

WILDER. [*Fretfully*] That may suit you, sir, but it doesn't suit me, or anyone else I should think.

                    [ANTHONY *looks him in the face—a silence*.

EDGAR. I don't see how we can get over it that to go on like this means starvation to the men's wives and families.

     [WILDER *turns abruptly to the fire, and* SCANTLEBURY *puts out a hand to push the idea away*.

WANKLIN. I'm afraid again that sounds a little sentimental.

EDGAR. Men of business are excused from decency, you think ?

WILDER. Nobody's more sorry for the men than I am, but if they [*lashing himself*] choose to be such a pig-headed lot, it's nothing to do with us ; we've quite enough on *our* hands to think of ourselves and the shareholders.

EDGAR. [*Irritably*] It won't kill the shareholders to miss a dividend or two ; I don't see that *that's* reason enough for knuckling under.

SCANTLEBURY. [*With grave discomfort*] You talk very lightly of your dividends, young man ; I don't know where we are.

WILDER. There's only one sound way of looking at it. We can't go on ruining *ourselves* with this strike.

ANTHONY. No caving in !

SCANTLEBURY. [*With a gesture of despair*] Look at him !

[ANTHONY *is leaning back in his chair. They do look at him.*

WILDER. [*Returning to his seat*] Well, all I can say is, if that's the Chairman's view, I don't know what we've come down here for.

ANTHONY. To tell the men that we've got nothing for them—— [*Grimly.*] They won't believe it till they hear it spoken in plain English.

WILDER. H'm ! Shouldn't be a bit surprised if that brute Roberts hadn't got us down here with the very same idea. I hate a man with a grievance.

EDGAR. [*Resentfully*] We didn't pay him enough for his discovery. I always said that at the time.

WILDER. We paid him five hundred and a bonus of two hundred three years later. If that's not enough ! What does he want for goodness' sake ?

TENCH. [*Complainingly*] Company made a hundred thousand out of his brains, and paid him seven hundred—that's the way he goes on, sir.

WILDER. The man's a rank agitator ! Look here, I hate the Unions. But now we've got Harness here let's get him to settle the whole thing.

ANTHONY. No !   [*Again they look at him.*

UNDERWOOD. Roberts won't let the men assent to that.

SCANTLEBURY. Fanatic ! Fanatic !

WILDER. [*Looking at* ANTHONY] And not the only one !

[FROST *enters from the hall.*

FROST. [*To* ANTHONY] Mr. Harness from the Union, waiting, sir. The men are here too, sir.

[ANTHONY *nods.* UNDERWOOD *goes to the door, returning with* HARNESS, *a pale, clean-shaven man with hollow cheeks, quick eyes and lantern jaw*—FROST *has retired.*

UNDERWOOD. [*Pointing to* TENCH's *chair*] Sit there next the Chairman, Harness, won't you ?

[*At* HARNESS's *appearance, the Board have drawn together, as it were, and turned a little to him, like cattle at a dog.*

HARNESS. [*With a sharp look round, and a bow*] Thanks ! [*He sits*

—*his accent is slightly nasal*.] Well, Gentlemen, we're going to do business at last, I hope.

WILDER. Depends on what you *call* business, Harness. Why don't you make the men come in ?

HARNESS. [*Sardonically*] The men are far more in the right than you are. The question with us is whether we shan't begin to support them again.

[*He ignores them all, except* ANTHONY, *to whom he turns in speaking.*

ANTHONY. Support them if you like ; we'll put in free labour and have done with it.

HARNESS. That won't do, Mr. Anthony. You can't get free labour, and you know it.

ANTHONY. We shall see that.

HARNESS. I'm quite frank with you. We were forced to withhold our support from your men because some of their demands are in excess of current rates. I expect to make them withdraw those demands to-day : if they do, take it straight from me, gentlemen, we shall back them again at once. Now, I want to see something fixed up before I go back to-night. Can't we have done with this old-fashioned tug-of-war business ? What good's it doing you ? Why don't you recognize once for all that these people are men like yourselves, and want what's good for them just as you want what's good for you—— [*Bitterly*.] Your motor-cars, and champagne, and eight-course dinners.

ANTHONY. If the men will come in, we'll do something for them.

HARNESS. [*Ironically*] Is that your opinion too, sir—and yours—and yours ? [*The Directors do not answer*.] Well, all I can say is : It's a kind of high and mighty aristocratic tone I thought we'd grown out of—seems I was mistaken.

ANTHONY. It's the tone the men use. Remains to be seen which can hold out longest—they without us, or we without them.

HARNESS. As business men, I wonder you're not ashamed of this waste of force, gentlemen. You know what it'll all end in.

ANTHONY. What ?

HARNESS. Compromise—it always does.

SCANTLEBURY. Can't you persuade the men that their interests are the same as ours ?

HARNESS. [*Turning ironically*] I could persuade them of that, sir, if they were.

WILDER. Come, Harness, you're a clever man, you don't believe all the Socialistic claptrap that's talked nowadays. There's no real difference between their interests and ours.

HARNESS. There's just one very simple little question I'd like to put to you. Will you pay your men one penny more than they force you to pay them ?   [WILDER *is silent.*

WANKLIN. [*Chiming in*] I humbly thought that not to pay more than was necessary was the A B C of commerce.

HARNESS. [*With irony*] Yes, that seems to be the A B C of commerce, sir ; and the A B C of commerce is between your interests and the men's.

SCANTLEBURY. [*Whispering*] We ought to arrange something.

HARNESS. [*Dryly*] Am I to understand then, gentlemen, that your Board is going to make no concessions ?

[WANKLIN *and* WILDER *bend forward as if to speak, but stop.*

ANTHONY. [*Nodding*] None.

[WANKLIN *and* WILDER *again bend forward, and* SCANTLEBURY *gives an unexpected grunt.*

HARNESS. You were about to say something, I believe ?

[*But* SCANTLEBURY *says nothing.*

EDGAR. [*Looking up suddenly*] We're sorry for the state of the men.

HARNESS. [*Icily*] The men have no use for your pity, sir. What they want is justice.

ANTHONY. Then let *them* be just.

HARNESS. For that word " just " read " humble," Mr. Anthony. Why should they be humble ? Barring the accident of money, aren't they as good men as you ?

ANTHONY. Cant !

HARNESS. Well, I've been five years in America. It colours a man's notions.

SCANTLEBURY. [*Suddenly, as though avenging his uncompleted grunt*] Let's have the men in and hear what they've got to say !

[ANTHONY *nods, and* UNDERWOOD *goes out by the single door.*

HARNESS. [*Dryly*] As I'm to have an interview with them this afternoon, gentlemen, I'll ask you to postpone your final decision till that's over.

[*Again* ANTHONY *nods, and taking up his glass drinks.*

[UNDERWOOD *comes in again, followed by* ROBERTS, GREEN, BULGIN, THOMAS, ROUS. *They file in, hat in hand, and stand silent in a row.* ROBERTS *is lean, of middle height, with a slight stoop. He has a little rat-gnawn, brown-grey beard, moustaches, high cheek-bones, hollow cheeks, small fiery eyes. He wears an old and grease-stained, blue serge suit, and carries an old bowler hat. He stands nearest the Chairman.* GREEN, *next to him, has a clean, worn face, with a small grey, goatee beard and drooping moustaches, iron spectacles, and mild, straightforward eyes. He wears an overcoat, green with age, and a linen collar. Next to him is* BULGIN, *a tall, strong man, with a dark moustache, and fighting jaw, wearing a red muffler, who keeps changing his cap from one hand to the other. Next to him is* THOMAS, *an old man with a grey moustache, full beard, and weatherbeaten, bony face, whose overcoat discloses a lean, plucked-looking neck. On his right,* ROUS, *the youngest of the five, looks like a soldier; he has a glitter in his eyes.*

UNDERWOOD. [*Pointing*] There are some chairs there against the wall, Roberts; won't you draw them up and sit down?

ROBERTS. Thank you, Mr. Underwood; we'll stand—in the presence of the Board. [*He speaks in a biting and staccato voice, rolling his r's, pronouncing his a's like an Italian a, and his consonants short and crisp.*] How are you, Mr. Harness? Didn't expect t' have the pleasure of seeing you till this afternoon.

HARNESS. [*Steadily*] We shall meet again then, Roberts.

ROBERTS. Glad to hear that; we shall have some news for you to take to your people.

ANTHONY. What do the men want?

ROBERTS. [*Acidly*] Beg pardon, I don't quite catch the Chairman's remark.

TENCH. [*From behind the Chairman's chair*] The Chairman wishes to know what the men have to say.

ROBERTS. It's what the Board has to say we've come to hear. It's for the Board to speak first.

ANTHONY. The Board has nothing to say.

ROBERTS. [*Looking along the line of men*] In that case we're wasting the Directors' time. We'll be taking our feet off this pretty carpet.

[*He turns, the men move slowly, as though hypnotically influenced.*

WANKLIN. [*Suavely*] Come, Roberts, you didn't give us this long cold journey for the pleasure of saying that.

THOMAS. [*A pure Welshman*] No, sir, an' what I say iss——

ROBERTS. [*Bitingly*] Go on, Henry Thomas, go on. You're better able to speak to the—Directors than me. [THOMAS *is silent.*

TENCH. The Chairman means, Roberts, that it was the men who asked for the Conference, the Board wish to hear what they have to say.

ROBERTS. Gad! If I was to begin to tell ye all they have to say, I wouldn't be finished to-day. And there'd be some that'd wish they'd never left their London palaces.

HARNESS. What's your proposition, man? Be reasonable.

ROBERTS. You want reason, Mr. Harness? Take a look round this afternoon before the meeting. [*He looks at the men; no sound escapes them.*] You'll see some very pretty scenery.

HARNESS. All right, my friend; you won't put me off.

ROBERTS. [*To the men*] We shan't put Mr. Harness off. Have some champagne with your lunch, Mr. Harness; you'll want it, sir.

HARNESS. Come, get to business, man!

THOMAS. What we're asking, look you, is just simple justice.

ROBERTS. [*Venomously*] Justice from London? What are you talking about, Henry Thomas? Have you gone silly? [THOMAS *is silent*.] We know very well what we are—discontented dogs—never satisfied. What did the Chairman tell me up in London? That I didn't know what I was talking about. I was a foolish, uneducated man, that knew nothing of the wants of the men I spoke for.

EDGAR. Do please keep to the point.

ANTHONY. [*Holding up his hand*] There can only be one master, Roberts.

ROBERTS. Then, be Gad, it'll be us.

[*There is a silence ;* ANTHONY *and* ROBERTS *stare at one another.*

UNDERWOOD. If you've nothing to say to the Directors, Roberts, perhaps you'll let Green or Thomas speak for the men.

[GREEN *and* THOMAS *look anxiously at* ROBERTS, *at each other, and the other men.*

GREEN. [*An Englishman*] If I'd been listened to, gentlemen——

THOMAS. What I'fe got to say iss what we'fe all got to say——

ROBERTS. Speak for yourself, Henry Thomas.

SCANTLEBURY. [*With a gesture of deep spiritual discomfort*] Let the poor men call their souls their own!

ROBERTS. Aye, they shall keep their souls, for it's not much body that you've left them, Mr. [*with biting emphasis, as though the word were an offence*] Scantlebury! [*To the men.*] Well, will you speak, or shall I speak for you?

ROUS. [*Suddenly*] Speak out, Roberts, or leave it to others.

ROBERTS. [*Ironically*] Thank you, George Rous. [*Addressing himself to* ANTHONY.] The Chairman and Board of Directors have honoured us by leaving London and coming all this way to hear what we've got to say; it would not be polite to keep them any longer waiting.

WILDER. Well, thank God for that !

ROBERTS. Ye will not dare to thank Him when I have done, Mr. Wilder, for all your piety. May be your God up in London has no time to listen to the working man. I'm told He is a wealthy God ; but if He listens to what I tell Him, He will know more than ever He learned in Kensington.

HARNESS. Come, Roberts, you have your own God. Respect the God of other men.

ROBERTS. That's right, sir. We have another God down here; I doubt He is rather different to Mr. Wilder's. Ask Henry Thomas ; he will tell you whether his God and Mr. Wilder's are the same.

[THOMAS *lifts his hand, and cranes his head as though to prophesy.*

WANKLIN. For goodness' sake, let's keep to the point, Roberts.

ROBERTS. I rather think it is the point, Mr. Wanklin. If you can get the God of Capital to walk through the streets of Labour, and pay attention to what he sees, you're a brighter man than I take you for, for all that you're a Radical.

ANTHONY. Attend to me, Roberts ! [ROBERTS *is silent.*] You are here to speak for the men, as I am here to speak for the Board.

[*He looks slowly round.*]

[WILDER, WANKLIN, *and* SCANTLEBURY *make movements of uneasiness, and* EDGAR *gazes at the floor. A faint smile comes on* HARNESS' *face.*]

Now then, what is it ?

ROBERTS. Right, sir !

[*Throughout all that follows, he and* ANTHONY *look fixedly upon each other. Men and Directors show in their various ways suppressed uneasiness, as though listening to words that they themselves would not have spoken.*]

The men can't afford to travel up to London ; and they don't trust you to believe what they say in black and white. They know what the post is [*he darts a look at* UNDERWOOD *and* TENCH], and what Directors' meetings are : " Refer it to the manager—let the manager advise us on the men's condition. Can we squeeze them a little more ? "

UNDERWOOD. [*In a low voice*] Don't hit below the belt, Roberts !

ROBERTS. Is it below the belt, Mr. Underwood ? The men know. When I came up to London, I told you the position straight. An' what came of it ? I was told I didn't know what I was talkin' about. I can't afford to travel up to London to be told that again.

ANTHONY. What have you to say for the men ?

ROBERTS. I have this to say—and first as to their condition. Ye shall 'ave no need to go and ask your manager. Ye can't squeeze them any more. Every man of us is well-nigh starving. [*A surprised murmur rises from the men.* ROBERTS *looks round.*] Ye wonder why I tell ye that ? Every man of us is going short. We can't be no worse off than we've been these weeks past. Ye needn't think that by waiting ye'll drive us to come in. We'll die first, the whole lot of us. The men have sent for ye to know, once and for all, whether ye are going to grant them their demands. I see the sheet of paper in the Secretary's hand. [TENCH *moves nervously.*] That's it, I think, Mr. Tench. It's not very large.

TENCH. [*Nodding*] Yes.

ROBERTS. There's not one sentence of writing on that paper that we can do without.

[*A movement amongst the men.* ROBERTS *turns on them sharply.*] Isn't that so ? "

[*The men assent reluctantly.* ANTHONY *takes from* TENCH *the paper and peruses it.*]

Not one single sentence. All those demands are fair. We have not asked anything that we are not entitled to ask. What I said up in London, I say again now : there is not anything on that piece of paper that a just man should not ask, and a just man give. [*A pause.*

ANTHONY. There is not one single demand on this paper that we will grant.

> [*In the stir that follows on these words,* ROBERTS *watches the Directors and* ANTHONY *the men.* WILDER *gets up abruptly and goes over to the fire.*

ROBERTS. D'ye mean that ?

ANTHONY. I do.

> [WILDER *at the fire makes an emphatic movement of disgust.*

ROBERTS. [*Noting it, with dry intensity*] Ye best know whether the condition of the Company is any better than the condition of the men. [*Scanning the Directors' faces.*] Ye best know whether ye can afford your tyranny—but this I tell ye : If ye think the men will give way the least part of an inch, ye're making the worst mistake ye ever made. [*He fixes his eyes on* SCANTLEBURY.] Ye think because the Union is not supporting us—more shame to it !—that we'll be coming on our knees to you one fine morning. Ye think because the men have got their wives an' families to think of—that it's just a question of a week or two——

ANTHONY. It would be better if you did not speculate so much on what we think.

ROBERTS. Aye ! It's not much profit to us ! I will say this for you, Mr. Anthony—ye know your own mind ! [*Staring at* ANTHONY.] I can reckon on ye !

ANTHONY. [*Ironically*] I am obliged to you !

ROBERTS. And I know mine. I tell ye this. The men will send their wives and families where the country will have to keep them ; an' they will starve sooner than give way. I advise ye, Mr. Anthony, to prepare yourself for the worst that can happen to your Company. We are not so ignorant as you might suppose. We know the way the cat is jumping. Your position is not all that it might be—not exactly !

ANTHONY. Be good enough to allow us to judge of our position for ourselves. Go back, and reconsider your own.

ROBERTS. [*Stepping forward*] Mr. Anthony, you are not a young man now ; from the time that I remember anything ye have been an enemy to every man that has come into your works. I don't say that ye're a mean man, or a cruel man, but ye've grudged them the say of any word in their own fate. Ye've fought them down four times. I've heard ye say ye love a fight—mark my words—ye're fighting the last fight ye'll ever fight——   [TENCH *touches* ROBERTS' *sleeve.*

UNDERWOOD. Roberts ! Roberts !

ROBERTS. Roberts ! Roberts ! I mustn't speak my mind to the Chairman, but the Chairman may speak his mind to me !

WILDER. What are things coming to ?

ANTHONY. [*With a grim smile at* WILDER] Go on, Roberts ; say what you like.

ROBERTS. [*After a pause*] I have no more to say.

ANTHONY. The meeting stands adjourned to five o'clock.

WANKLIN. [*In a low voice to* UNDERWOOD] We shall never settle anything like this.

ROBERTS. [*Bitingly*] We thank the Chairman and Board of Directors for their gracious hearing.

[*He moves towards the door ; the men cluster together stupefied ; then* ROUS, *throwing up his head, passes* ROBERTS *and goes out. The others follow.*

ROBERTS. [*With his hand on the door—maliciously*] Good day, gentlemen ! [*He goes out.*

HARNESS. [*Ironically*] I congratulate you on the conciliatory spirit that's been displayed. With your permission, gentlemen, I'll be with you again at half-past five. Good morning !

[*He bows slightly, rests his eyes on* ANTHONY, *who returns his stare unmoved, and, followed by* UNDERWOOD, *goes out. There is a moment of uneasy silence.* UNDERWOOD *reappears in the doorway.*

WILDER. [*With emphatic disgust*] Well !

[*The double doors are opened.*

ENID. [*Standing in the doorway*] Lunch is ready.

[EDGAR, *getting up abruptly, walks out past his sister.*

WILDER. Coming to lunch, Scantlebury ?

SCANTLEBURY. [*Rising heavily*] I suppose so, I suppose so. It's the only thing we can do. [*They go out through the double doors.*

WANKLIN. [*In a low voice*] Do you really mean to fight to a finish, Chairman ? [ANTHONY *nods.*

WANKLIN. Take care ! The essence of things is to know when to stop. [ANTHONY *does not answer.*

WANKLIN. [*Very gravely*] This way disaster lies. The ancient Trojans were fools to your father, Mrs. Underwood.

[*He goes out through the double doors.*

ENID. I want to speak to father, Frank.

[UNDERWOOD *follows* WANKLIN *out.* TENCH, *passing round the table, is restoring order to the scattered pens and papers.*

ENID. Aren't you coming, Dad ?

[ANTHONY *shakes his head.* ENID *looks meaningly at* TENCH.

ENID. Won't you go and have some lunch, Mr. Tench.

TENCH. [*With papers in his hand*] Thank you, ma'am, thank you !

[*He goes slowly, looking back.*

ENID. [*Shutting the doors*] I *do* hope it's settled, father!

ANTHONY. No!

ENID. [*Very disappointed*] Oh! Haven't you done anything?

[ANTHONY *shakes his head.*

ENID. Frank says they all want to come to a compromise, really, except that man Roberts.

ANTHONY. *I* don't.

ENID. It's such a horrid position for us. If you were the wife of the manager, and lived down here, and saw it all. You can't realize, Dad!

ANTHONY. Indeed?

ENID. We see *all* the distress. You remember my maid Annie, who married Roberts? [ANTHONY *nods.*] It's so wretched, her heart's weak; since the strike began, she hasn't even been getting proper food. I know it for a fact, father.

ANTHONY. Give her what she wants, poor woman!

ENID. Roberts won't let her take anything from *us.*

ANTHONY. [*Staring before him*] I can't be answerable for the men's obstinacy.

ENID. They're all suffering. Father! Do stop it, for my sake!

ANTHONY. [*With a keen look at her*] You don't understand, my dear.

ENID. If I were on the Board, I'd do something.

ANTHONY. What would you do?

ENID. It's because you can't bear to give way. It's so——

ANTHONY. Well?

ENID. So unnecessary.

ANTHONY. What do *you* know about necessity? Read your novels, play your music, talk your talk, but don't try and tell *me* what's at the bottom of a struggle like this.

ENID. I live down here, and see it.

ANTHONY. What d'you imagine stands between you and your class and these men that you're so sorry for?

ENID. [*Coldly*] I don't know what you mean, father.

ANTHONY. In a few years you and your children would be down in the condition they're in, but for those who have the eyes to see things as they are and the backbone to stand up for themselves.

ENID. You don't know the state the men are in.

ANTHONY. I know it well enough.

ENID. You don't, father; if you did, you wouldn't——

ANTHONY. It's you who don't know the simple facts of the position. What sort of mercy do you suppose you'd get if no one stood between you and the continual demands of labour? This sort of mercy— [*he puts his hand up to his throat and squeezes it.*] First would go your sentiments, my dear; then your culture, and your comforts would be going all the time!

ENID. I don't believe in barriers between classes.

ANTHONY. You — don't — believe — in — barriers — between the classes ?

ENID. [*Coldly*] And I don't know what that has to do with this question.

ANTHONY. It will take a generation or two for you to understand.

ENID. It's only you and Roberts, father, and you know it!

[ANTHONY *thrusts out his lower lip.*]

It'll ruin the Company.

ANTHONY. Allow me to judge of that.

ENID. [*Resentfully*] I won't stand by and let poor Annie Roberts suffer like this ! And think of the children, father ! I warn you.

ANTHONY. [*With a grim smile*] What do you propose to do ?

ENID. That's my affair. [ANTHONY *only looks at her.*

ENID. [*In a changed voice, stroking his sleeve*] Father, you *know* you oughtn't to have this strain on you—you know what Dr. Fisher said !

ANTHONY. No old man can afford to listen to old women.

ENID. But you *have* done enough, even if it really is such a matter of principle with you.

ANTHONY. You think so ?

ENID. Don't, Dad ! [*Her face works.*] You—you might think of *us* !

ANTHONY. I am.

ENID. It'll break you down.

ANTHONY. [*Slowly*] My dear, I am not going to funk ; you may rely on that.

[*Re-enter* TENCH *with papers ; he glances at them, then plucking up courage.*

TENCH. Beg pardon, Madam, I think I'd rather see these papers were disposed of before I get my lunch.

[ENID, *after an impatient glance at him, looks at her father, turns suddenly, and goes into the drawing-room.*

TENCH. [*Holding the papers and a pen to* ANTHONY, *very nervously*] Would you sign these for me, please sir ?

[ANTHONY *takes the pen and signs.*

TENCH. [*Standing with a sheet of blotting-paper behind* EDGAR'S *chair, begins speaking nervously*] I owe my position to you, sir.

ANTHONY. Well ?

TENCH. I'm obliged to see everything that's going on, sir ; I—I depend upon the Company entirely. If anything were to happen to it, it'd be disastrous for me. [ANTHONY *nods.*] And, of course, my wife's just had another ; and so it makes me doubly anxious just now. And the rates are really terrible down our way.

ANTHONY. [*With grim amusement*] Not more terrible than they are up mine.

TENCH. No, sir? [*Very nervously.*] I know the Company means a great deal to you, sir.

ANTHONY. It does; I founded it.

TENCH. Yes, sir. If the strike goes on it'll be very serious. I think the Directors are beginning to realize that, sir.

ANTHONY. [*Ironically*] Indeed?

TENCH. I know you hold very strong views, sir, and it's always your habit to look things in the face; but I don't think the Directors —like it, sir, now they—they see it.

ANTHONY. [*Grimly*] Nor you, it seems.

TENCH. [*With the ghost of a smile*] No, sir; of course I've got my children, and my wife's delicate; in my position I *have* to think of these things. [ANTHONY *nods.*] It wasn't *that* I was going to say, sir, if you'll excuse me [*hesitates*]——

ANTHONY. Out with it, then!

TENCH. I know—from my own father, sir, that when you get on in life you do feel things dreadfully——

ANTHONY. [*Almost paternally*] Come, out with it, Tench!

TENCH. I don't *like* to say it, sir.

ANTHONY. [*Stonily*] You must.

TENCH. [*After a pause, desperately bolting it out*] I think the Directors are going to throw you over, sir.

ANTHONY. [*Sits in silence*] Ring the bell!

[TENCH *nervously rings the bell and stands by the fire.*

TENCH. Excuse me saying such a thing. I was *only* thinking of you, sir.

[FROST *enters from the hall, he comes to the foot of the table, and looks at* ANTHONY; TENCH *covers his nervousness by arranging papers.*

ANTHONY. Bring me a whisky and soda.

FROST. Anything to eat, sir?

[ANTHONY *shakes his head*—FROST *goes to the sideboard, and prepares the drink.*

TENCH. [*In a low voice, almost supplicating*] If you *could* see your way, sir, it would be a great relief to my mind, it would indeed. [*He looks up at* ANTHONY, *who has not moved.*] It does make me so very anxious. I haven't slept properly for weeks, sir, and that's a fact.

[ANTHONY *looks in his face, then slowly shakes his head.*

TENCH. [*Disheartened*] No, sir? [*He goes on arranging papers.* FROST *places the whisky and soda on a salver and puts it down by* ANTHONY'S *right hand. He stands away, looking gravely at* ANTHONY.

FROST. *Nothing* I can get you, sir? [ANTHONY *shakes his head.*] You're aware, sir, of what the doctor said, sir?

ANTHONY. I am.

[*A pause.* FROST *suddenly moves closer to him, and speaks in a low voice.*

FROST. This strike, sir; puttin' all this strain on you. Excuse me, sir, is it—is it worth it, sir?

[ANTHONY *mutters some words that are inaudible.*]

Very good, sir!

> [*He turns and goes out into the hall*—TENCH *makes two attempts to speak; but meeting his Chairman's gaze he drops his eyes, and turning dismally, he too goes out.* ANTHONY *is left alone. He grips the glass, tilts it, and drinks deeply; then sets it down with a deep and rumbling sigh, and leans back in his chair.*

The curtain falls.

ACT II

SCENE I

It is half-past three. In the kitchen of ROBERTS' *cottage a meagre little fire is burning. The room is clean and tidy, very barely furnished, with a brick floor and white-washed walls, much stained with smoke. There is a kettle on the fire. A door opposite the fireplace opens inwards from a snowy street. On the wooden table are a cup and saucer, a teapot, knife, and plate of bread and cheese. Close to the fireplace in an old armchair, wrapped in a rug, sits* MRS. ROBERTS, *a thin and dark-haired woman about thirty-five, with patient eyes. Her hair is not done up, but tied back with a piece of ribbon. By the fire, too, is* MRS. YEO; *a red-haired, broad-faced person. Sitting near the table is* MRS. ROUS, *an old lady, ashen-white, with silver hair; by the door, standing, as if about to go, is* MRS. BULGIN, *a little pale, pinched-up woman. In a chair, with her elbows resting on the table, and her face resting in her hands sits* MADGE THOMAS, *a good-looking girl, of twenty-two, with high cheekbones, deep-set eyes, and dark, untidy hair. She is listening to the talk but she neither speaks nor moves.*

MRS. YEO. So he give me a sixpence, and that's the first bit o' money *I* seen this week. There an't much 'eat to this fire. Come and warm yerself, Mrs. Rous, you're lookin' as white as the snow, you are.

MRS. ROUS. [*Shivering—placidly*] Ah! but the winter my old man was took was the proper winter. Seventy-nine that was, when none of you was hardly born—not Madge Thomas, nor Sue Bulgin. [*Looking at them in turn.*] Annie Roberts, 'ow old were you, dear?

MRS. ROBERTS. Seven, Mrs. Rous.

MRS. ROUS. Seven—well ther'! A tiny little thing!

MRS. YEO. [*Aggressively*] Well, I was ten myself, *I* remembers it.

MRS. ROUS. [*Placidly*] The Company hadn't been started three years. Father was workin' on the acid that's 'ow he got 'is pisoned leg. I kep' sayin' to 'im "Father, you've got a pisoned leg." "Well," 'e, said, "Mother, pison or no pison, I can't afford to go a-layin' up." An' two days after he was on 'is back, and never got up again. It was Providence! There wasn't none o' these Compension Acts then.

MRS. YEO. Ye hadn't no strike that winter! [*With grim humour.*] This winter's 'ard enough for me. Mrs. Roberts, you don't want no

19

'arder winter, do you? Wouldn't seem natural to 'ave a dinner, would it, Mrs. Bulgin?

MRS. BULGIN. We've had bread and tea last four days.

MRS. YEO. You got that Friday's laundry job?

MRS. BULGIN. [*Dispiritedly*] They said they'd give it me, but when I went last Friday, they were full up. I got to go again next week.

MRS. YEO. Ah! There's too many after that. I send Yeo out on the ice to put on the gentry's skates an' pick up what 'e can. Stops 'im from broodin' about the 'ouse.

MRS. BULGIN. [*In a desolate, matter-of-fact voice*] Leavin' out the men—it's bad enough with the children. I keep 'em in bed, they don't get so hungry when they're not running about; but they're that restless in bed they worry your life out.

MRS. YEO. You're lucky they're all so small. It's the goin' to school that makes 'em 'ungry. Don't Bulgin give you *anythin'*?

MRS. BULGIN. [*Shakes her head, then, as though by afterthought*] Would if he could, I s'pose.

MRS. YEO. [*Sardonically*] What! 'Aven't 'e got no shares in the Company?

MRS. ROUS. [*Rising with tremendous cheerfulness*] Well, good-bye, Annie Roberts, I'm going along home.

MRS. ROBERTS. Stay an' have a cup of tea, Mrs. Rous?

MRS. ROUS. [*With the faintest smile*] Roberts'll want 'is tea when he comes in. I'll just go an' get to bed; it's warmer there than anywhere.

[*She moves very shakily towards the door*.

MRS. YEO. [*Rising and giving her an arm*] Come on, Mother, take my arm; we're all goin' the same way.

MRS. ROUS. [*Taking the arm*] Thank you, my dearies!

[*They go out, followed by* MRS. BULGIN.

MADGE. [*Moving for the first time*] There, Annie, you see that! I told George Rous, "Don't think to have my company till you've made an end of all this trouble. You ought to be ashamed," I said, "with your own mother looking like a ghost, and not a stick to put on the fire. So long as you're able to fill your pipes, you'll let us starve." "I'll take my oath, Madge," he said, "I've not had smoke nor drink these three weeks!" "Well, then, why do you go on with it?" "I can't go back on Roberts!" . . . That's it! Roberts, always Roberts! They'd all drop it but for him. When *he* talks it's the devil that comes into them.

[*A silence.* MRS. ROBERTS *makes a movement of pain.*] Ah! *You* don't want him beaten! He's your man. With everybody like their own shadows! [*She makes a gesture towards* MRS. ROBERTS.] If Rous wants me he must give up Roberts. If *he* gave him up—they all would. They're only waiting for a lead. Father's against him —they're all against him in their hearts.

MRS. ROBERTS. You won't beat Roberts! [*They look silently at each other.*]

MADGE. Won't I? The cowards—when their own mothers and their own children don't know where to turn.

MRS. ROBERTS. Madge!

MADGE. [*Looking searchingly at* MRS. ROBERTS] I wonder he can look *you* in the face. [*She squats before the fire, with her hands out to the flame.*] Harness is here again. They'll have to make up their minds to-day.

MRS. ROBERTS. [*In a soft, slow voice, with a slight West-country burr*] Roberts will never give up the furnacemen and engineers. 'Twouldn't be right.

MADGE. You can't deceive me. It's just his pride.

> [*A tapping at the door is heard, the women turn as* ENID *enters. She wears a round fur cap, and a jacket of squirrel's fur. She closes the door behind her.*

ENID. Can I come in, Annie?

MRS. ROBERTS. [*Flinching*] Miss Enid! Give Mrs. Underwood a chair, Madge.   [MADGE *gives* ENID *the chair she has been sitting on.*

ENID. Thank you!

ENID. Are you any better?

MRS. ROBERTS. Yes, M'm; thank you, M'm.

ENID. [*Looking at the sullen* MADGE *as though requesting her departure*] Why did you send back the jelly? I call that really wicked of you!

MRS. ROBERTS. Thank you, M'm, I'd no need for it.

ENID. Of course! It was Roberts' doing, wasn't it? How can he let all this suffering go on amongst you?

MADGE. [*Suddenly*] What suffering?

ENID. [*Surprised*] I beg your pardon!

MADGE. Who said there was suffering?

MRS. ROBERTS. Madge!

MADGE. [*Throwing her shawl over her head*] Please to let us keep ourselves to ourselves. We don't want you coming here and spying on us.

ENID. [*Confronting her, but without rising*] I didn't speak to you.

MADGE. [*In a low, fierce voice*] Keep your kind feelings to yourself. You think you can come amongst us, but you're mistaken. Go back and tell the Manager that.

ENID. [*Stonily*] This is not your house.

MADGE. [*Turning to the door*] No, it is not my house; keep clear of my house, Mrs. Underwood.

> [*She goes out.* ENID *taps her fingers on the table.*

MRS. ROBERTS. Please to forgive Madge Thomas, M'm; she's a bit upset to-day.   [*A pause.*

ENID. [*Looking at her*] Oh, I think they're so *stupid*, all of them.

5

MRS. ROBERTS. [*With a faint smile*] Yes, M'm.

ENID. Is Roberts out?

MRS. ROBERTS. Yes, M'm.

ENID. It is *his doing*, that they don't come to an agreement. Now isn't it, Annie?

MRS. ROBERTS. [*Softly, with her eyes on* ENID, *and moving the fingers of one hand continually on her breast*] They do say that your father, M'm——

ENID. My father's getting an old man, and you know what old men are.

MRS. ROBERTS. I am sorry, M'm.

ENID. [*More softly*] I don't expect *you* to feel sorry, Annie. I know it's his fault as well as Roberts'.

MRS. ROBERTS. I'm sorry for anyone that gets old, M'm; it's dreadful to get old, and Mr. Anthony was such a fine old man I always used to think.

ENID. [*Impulsively*] He always liked you, don't you remember? Look here, Annie, what can I do? I do so want to know. You don't get what you ought to have. [*Going to the fire, she takes the kettle off, and looks for coals.*] And you're so naughty sending back the soup and things!

MRS. ROBERTS. [*With a faint smile*] Yes, M'm?

ENID. [*Resentfully*] Why, you haven't even got coals?

MRS. ROBERTS. If you please, M'm, to put the kettle on again; Roberts won't have long for his tea when he comes in. He's got to meet the men at four.

ENID. [*Putting the kettle on*] That means he'll lash them into a fury again. Can't you stop his going, Annie? [MRS. ROBERTS *smiles ironically.*] Have you tried? [*A silence.*] Does he know how ill you are?

MRS. ROBERTS. It's only my weak 'eart, M'm.

ENID. You used to be so well when you were with us.

MRS. ROBERTS. [*Stiffening*] Roberts is always good to me.

ENID. But you ought to have everything you want, and you have nothing!

MRS. ROBERTS. [*Appealingly*] They tell me I don't look like a dyin' woman?

ENID. Of course you don't; if you could only have proper—— Will you see my doctor if I send him to you? I'm sure he'd do you good.

MRS. ROBERTS. [*With faint questioning*] Yes, M'm.

ENID. Madge Thomas oughtn't to come here; she only excites you. As if I didn't know what suffering there is amongst the men! I do feel for them dreadfully, but you know they *have* gone too far.

MRS. ROBERTS. [*Continually moving her fingers*] They say there's no other way to get better wages, M'm.

ENID. [*Earnestly*] But, Annie, that's why the Union won't help them. My husband's very sympathetic with the men, but he says they're not underpaid.

MRS. ROBERTS. No, M'm?

ENID. They never think how the Company could go on if we paid the wages they want.

MRS. ROBERTS. [*With an effort*] But the dividends having been so big, M'm.

ENID. [*Taken aback*] You all seem to think the shareholders are rich men, but they're not—most of them are really no better off than working men. [MRS. ROBERTS *smiles.*] They have to keep up appearances.

MRS. ROBERTS. Yes, M'm?

ENID. You don't have to pay rates and taxes, and a hundred other things that they do. If the men didn't spend such a lot in drink and betting they'd be quite well off!

MRS. ROBERTS. They say, workin' so hard, they must have some pleasure.

ENID. But surely not low pleasure like that.

MRS. ROBERTS. [*A little resentfully*] Roberts never touches a drop; and he's never had a bet in his life.

ENID. Oh! but he's not a com—— I mean he's an engineer— a superior man.

MRS. ROBERTS. Yes, M'm. Roberts says they've no chance of other pleasures.

ENID. [*Musing*] Of course, I know it's hard.

MRS. ROBERTS. [*With a spice of malice*] And they say gentlefolk's just as bad.

ENID. [*With a smile*] I go as far as most people, Annie, but you know, yourself, that's nonsense.

MRS. ROBERTS. [*With painful effort*] A lot o' the men never go near the Public; but even they don't save but very little, and that goes if there's illness.

ENID. But they've got their clubs, haven't they?

MRS. ROBERTS. The clubs only give up to eighteen shillin's a week, M'm, and it's not much amongst a family. Roberts says workin' folk have always lived from hand to mouth. Sixpence to-day is worth more than a shillin' to-morrow, that's what they say.

ENID. But that's the spirit of gambling.

MRS. ROBERTS. [*With a sort of excitement*] Roberts says a working man's life is all a gamble, from the time 'e's born to the time 'e dies.

      [ENID *leans forward, interested.* MRS. ROBERTS *goes on with a growing excitement that culminates in the personal feeling of the last words.*]

He says, M'm, that when a working man's baby is born, it's a toss-up from breath to breath whether it ever draws another, and so on all 'is life ; an' when he comes to be old, it's the workhouse or the grave. He says that without a man is very near, and pinches and stints 'imself and 'is children to save, there can't be neither surplus nor security.   That's why he wouldn't have no children [*she sinks back*], not though I *wanted* them.

ENID. Yes, yes, I know !

MRS. ROBERTS. No, you don't, M'm.   You've got your children, and you'll never need to trouble for them.

ENID. [*Gently*] You oughtn't to be talking so much, Annie. [*Then, in spite of herself.*] But Roberts was paid a lot of money, wasn't he, for discovering that process ?

MRS. ROBERTS. [*On the defensive*] All Roberts' savin's have gone. He's always looked forward to this strike.   He says he's no right to a farthing when the others are suffering.   'Tisn't so with all o' them ! Some don't seem to care no more than that—so long as they get their own.

ENID. I don't see how they can be expected to when they're suffering like this. [*In a changed voice.*] But Roberts ought to think of *you !*   It's all terrible !   The kettle's boiling.   Shall I make the tea ? [*She takes the teapot, and seeing tea there, pours water into it.*] Won't you have a cup ?

MRS. ROBERTS. No, thank you, M'm. [*She is listening, as though for footsteps.*] I'd sooner you didn't see Roberts, M'm, he gets so wild.

ENID. Oh ! but I must, Annie ; I'll be quite calm, I promise.

MRS. ROBERTS. It's life an' death to him, M'm.

ENID. [*Very gently*] I'll get him to talk to me outside, we won't excite you.

MRS. ROBERTS. [*Faintly*] No, M'm.

                    [*She gives a violent start. ROBERTS has come in, unseen.*

ROBERTS. [*Removing his hat—with subtle mockery*] Beg pardon for coming in ; you're engaged with a lady, I see.

ENID. Can I speak to you, Mr. Roberts ?

ROBERTS. Whom have I the pleasure of addressing, Ma'am ?

ENID. But surely you know me !   I'm Mrs. Underwood.

ROBERTS. [*With a bow of malice*] The daughter of our chairman.

ENID [*Earnestly*] I've come on purpose to speak to you ; will you come outside a minute ?   [*She looks at MRS. ROBERTS.*

ROBERTS. [*Hanging up his hat*] I have nothing to say, Ma'am.

ENID. But I *must* speak to you, please.   [*She moves towards the door.*

ROBERTS. [*With sudden venom*] I have not the time to listen !

MRS. ROBERTS. David !

ENID. Mr. Roberts, *please !*

ROBERTS. [*Taking off his overcoat*] I am sorry to disoblige a lady— Mr. Anthony's daughter.

ENID. [*Wavering, then with sudden decision*] Mr. Roberts, I know you've another meeting of the men.   [ROBERTS *bows*.] I came to appeal to you.   Please, please try to come to some compromise ; give way a little, if it's only for your own sakes !

ROBERTS. [*Speaking to himself*] The daughter of Mr. Anthony begs me to give way a little, if it's only for our own sakes.

ENID. For everybody's sake ; for your wife's sake.

ROBERTS. For my wife's sake, for everybody's sake—for the sake of Mr. Anthony.

ENID. Why are you so bitter against my father ?   He has never done anything to you.

ROBERTS. Has he not ?

ENID. He can't help his views, any more than you can help yours.

ROBERTS. I really didn't know that I had a right to views !

ENID. He's an old man, and you——
                              [*Seeing his eyes fixed on her, she stops.*

ROBERTS. [*Without raising his voice*] If I saw Mr. Anthony going to die, and I could save him by lifting my hand, I would not lift the little finger of it.

ENID. You—you——   [*She stops again, biting her lips.*

ROBERTS. I would not, and that's flat !

ENID. [*Coldly*] You don't mean what you say, and you know it !

ROBERTS. I mean every word of it.

ENID. But why ?

ROBERTS. [*With a flash*] Mr. Anthony stands for tyranny !   That's why !

ENID. Nonsense !

     [MRS. ROBERTS *makes a movement as if to rise, but sinks back in
      her chair.*

ENID. [*With an impetuous movement*] Annie !

ROBERTS. Please not to touch my wife !

ENID. [*Recoiling with a sort of horror*] I believe—you are mad.

ROBERTS. The house of a madman then is not the fit place for a lady.

ENID. I'm not afraid of you.

ROBERTS. [*Bowing*] I would not expect the daughter of Mr. Anthony to be afraid.   Mr. Anthony is not a coward like the rest of them.

ENID. [*Suddenly*] I suppose you think it brave, then, to go on with this struggle.

ROBERTS. Does Mr. Anthony think it brave to fight against women and children ?   Mr. Anthony is a rich man, I believe ; does he think it brave to fight against those who haven't a penny ?   Does he think it brave to set children crying with hunger, an' women shivering with cold ?

ENID. [*Putting up her hand, as though warding off a blow*] My father is acting on his principles, and you know it!

ROBERTS. And so am I!

ENID. You hate us; and you can't bear to be beaten.

ROBERTS. Neither can Mr. Anthony, for all that he may say.

ENID. At any rate you might have pity on your wife.

[MRS. ROBERTS, *who has her hand pressed to her heart, takes it away, and tries to calm her breathing.*

ROBERTS. Madam, I have no more to say.

[*He takes up the loaf. There is a knock at the door, and* UNDER-WOOD *comes in. He stands looking at them,* ENID *turns to him, then seems undecided.*

UNDERWOOD. Enid!

ROBERTS. [*Ironically*] Ye were not needing to come for your wife, Mr. Underwood. We are not rowdies.

UNDERWOOD. I know that, Roberts. I hope Mrs. Roberts is better.

[ROBERTS *turns away without answering.*]

Come, Enid!

ENID. I make one more appeal to you, Mr. Roberts, for the sake of your wife.

ROBERTS. [*With polite malice*] If I might advise ye, Ma'am—make it for the sake of your husband and your father.

[ENID, *suppressing a retort, goes out.* UNDERWOOD *opens the door for her and follows.* ROBERTS, *going to the fire, holds out his hands to the dying glow.*

ROBERTS. How goes it, my girl? Feeling better, are you?

[MRS. ROBERTS *smiles faintly. He brings his overcoat and wraps it round her.*]

[*Looking at his watch.*] Ten minutes to four! [*As though inspired.*] I've seen their faces, there's no fight in them, except for that one old robber.

MRS. ROBERTS. Won't you stop and eat, David? You've 'ad nothing all day!

ROBERTS. [*Putting his hand to his throat*] Can't swallow till those old sharks are out o' the town. [*He walks up and down.*] I shall have a bother with the men—there's no heart in them, the cowards. Blind as bats, they are—can't see a day before their noses.

MRS. ROBERTS. It's the women, David.

ROBERTS. Ah! So they say! They can remember the women when their own bellies speak! The women never stops them from the drink; but from a little suffering to themselves in a sacred cause, the women stop them fast enough.

MRS. ROBERTS. But think o' the children, David.

ROBERTS. Ah! If they will go breeding themselves for slaves, without a thought o' the future o' them they breed——

MRS. ROBERTS. [*Gasping*] That's enough, David; don't begin to talk of that—I won't—I can't——

ROBERTS. [*Staring at her*] Now, now, my girl!

MRS. ROBERTS. [*Breathlessly*] No, no, David—I won't!

ROBERTS. There, there! Come, come! That's right. [*Bitterly.*] Not one penny will they put by for a day like this. Not they! Hand to mouth—Gad!—I know them! They've broke my heart. There was no holdin' them at the start, but now the pinch 'as come.

MRS. ROBERTS. How can you expect it, David? They're not made of iron.

ROBERTS. Expect it? Wouldn't I expect what I would do meself? Wouldn't I starve an' rot rather than give in? What one man can do, another can.

MRS. ROBERTS. And the women?

ROBERTS. This is not women's work.

MRS. ROBERTS. [*With a flash of malice*] No, the women may die for all you care. That's their work.

ROBERTS. [*Averting his eyes*] Who talks of dying? No one will die till we have beaten these——

      [*He meets her eyes again, and again turns his away. Excitedly.*] This is what I've been waiting for all these months. To get the old robbers down, and send them home again without a farthin's worth o' change. I've seen their faces, I tell you, in the valley of the shadow of defeat.   [*He goes to the peg and takes down his hat.*

MRS. ROBERTS. [*Following with her eyes—softly*] Take your overcoat, David; it must be bitter cold.

ROBERTS. [*Coming up to her—his eyes are furtive*] No, no! There, there, stay quiet and warm. I won't be long, my girl!

MRS. ROBERTS. [*With soft bitterness*] You'd better take it.

      [*She lifts the coat. But* ROBERTS *puts it back, and wraps it round her. He tries to meet her eyes, but cannot.* MRS. ROBERTS *stays huddled in the coat, her eyes, that follow him about, are half malicious, half yearning. He looks at his watch again, and turns to go. In the doorway he meets* JAN THOMAS, *a boy of ten in clothes too big for him, carrying a penny whistle.*

ROBERTS. Hallo, boy!

      [*He goes,* JAN *stops within a yard of* MRS. ROBERTS, *and stares at her without a word.*

MRS. ROBERTS. Well, Jan!

JAN. Father's coming; sister Madge is coming.

      [*He sits at the table, and fidgets with his whistle; he blows three vague notes; then imitates a cuckoo.*

      [*There is a tap on the door. Old* THOMAS *comes in.*

THOMAS. A very coot tay to you, Ma'am. It is petter that you are.

MRS. ROBERTS. Thank you, Mr. Thomas.

THOMAS. [*Nervously*] Roberts in ?

MRS. ROBERTS. Just gone on to the meeting, Mr. Thomas.

THOMAS. [*With relief, becoming talkative*] This is fery unfortunate, look you ! I came to tell him that we must make terms with London. It is a fery great pity he is gone to the meeting. He will be kicking against the pricks, I am thinking.

MRS. ROBERTS. [*Half rising*] He'll never give in, Mr. Thomas.

THOMAS. You must not be fretting, that is very pat for you. Look you, there iss hartly any mans for supporting him now, but the engineers and George Rous. [*Solemnly.*] This strike is no longer coing with Chapel, look you ! I have listened carefully, an' I have talked with her. [JAN *blows.*] Sst ! I don't care what th' others say, I say that *Chapel means us* to be stopping the trouble, that is what I make of her ; and it is my opinion that this is the fery best thing for all of us. If it wasn't my opinion, I ton't say—but it is my opinion, look you.

MRS. ROBERTS. [*Trying to suppress her excitement*] I don't know what'll come to Roberts, if you give in.

THOMAS. It iss no disgrace whateffer ! All that a mortal man coult do he hass tone. It iss against Human Nature he hass gone ; fery natural—any man may to that ; but Chapel has spoken and he must not co against *her*.   [JAN *imitates the cuckoo.*] Ton't make that squeaking ! [*Going to the door.*] Here iss my taughter come to sit with you. A fery goot day, Ma'am—no fretting—rememper !

[MADGE *comes in and stands at the open door, watching the street.*

MADGE. You'll be late, Father ; they're beginning. [*She catches him by the sleeve.*] For the love of God, stand up to him, Father—this time !

THOMAS. [*Detaching his sleeve with dignity*] Leave me to do what's proper, girl !

[*He goes out,* MADGE, *in the centre of the open doorway, slowly moves in, as though before the approach of someone.*

ROUS. [*Appearing in the doorway*] Madge !

[MADGE *stands with her back to* MRS. ROBERTS, *staring at him with her head up and her hands behind her.*

ROUS. [*Who has a fierce distracted look*] Madge ! I'm going to the meeting.

[MADGE, *without moving, smiles contemptuously.*]
D'ye hear me ?   [*They speak in quick low voices.*

MADGE. I hear ! Go, and kill your own Mother, if you must.

[ROUS *seizes her by both her arms. She stands rigid, with her head bent back. He releases her, and he too stands motionless.*

ROUS. I swore to stand by Roberts. I swore that ! Ye want me to go back on what I've sworn.

MADGE. [*With slow soft mockery*] You are a pretty lover !

Rous. Madge !

MADGE. [*Smiling*] I've heard that lovers do what their girls ask them
—[JAN *sounds the cuckoo's notes*]—but that's not true, it seems !

Rous. You'd make a blackleg of me !

MADGE. [*With her eyes half-closed*] Do it for me !

Rous. [*Dashing his hand across his brow*] Damn ! I can't !

MADGE. [*Swiftly*] Do it for me !

Rous. [*Through his teeth*] Don't play the wanton with me !

MADGE. [*With a movement of her hand towards* JAN—*quick and low*]
I'd do *that* to get the children bread !

Rous. [*In a fierce whisper*] Madge ! Oh, Madge !

MADGE. [*With soft mockery*] But *you* can't break your word with me !

Rous. [*With a choke*] Then, Begod, I can !

[*He turns and rushes off.*

[MADGE *stands with a faint smile on her face, looking after him.
She moves to the table.*

MADGE. I have done for Roberts !

[*She sees that* MRS. ROBERTS *has sunk back in her chair.*

MADGE. [*Running to her, and feeling her hands*] You're as cold as a
stone ! You want a drop of brandy. Jan, run to the " Lion " ; say
I sent you for Mrs. Roberts.

MRS. ROBERTS. [*With a feeble movement*] I'll just sit quiet, Madge.
Give Jan—his—tea.

MADGE. [*Giving* JAN *a slice of bread*] There, ye little rascal. Hold
your piping. [*Going to the fire, she kneels.*] It's going out.

MRS. ROBERTS. [*With a faint smile*] 'Tis all the same !

[JAN *begins to blow his whistle.*

MADGE. Tsht ! Tsht !—you——   [JAN *stops.*

MRS. ROBERTS. [*Smiling*] Let 'im play, Madge.

MADGE. [*On her knees at the fire, listening*] Waiting an' waiting.
I've no patience with it ; waiting an' waiting—that's what a woman
has to do ! Can you hear them at it—I can !

[*She leans her elbows on the table, and her chin on her hands. Behind
her,* MRS. ROBERTS *leans forward, with painful and growing
excitement, as the sounds of the strikers' meeting come in.*

The curtain falls.

SCENE II

*It is past four. In a grey, failing light, an open muddy space is crowded with
workmen. Beyond, divided from it by a barbed-wire fence, is the raised
towing-path of a canal, on which is moored a barge. In the distance are
marshes and snow-covered hills. The " Works' " high wall runs from*

the canal across the open space, and in the angle of this wall is a rude platform of barrels and boards. On it, HARNESS is standing. ROBERTS, a little apart from the crowd, leans his back against the wall. On the raised towing-path two bargemen lounge and smoke indifferently.

HARNESS. [*Holding out his hand*] Well, I've spoken to you straight. If I speak till to-morrow I can't say more.

JAGO. [*A dark, sallow, Spanish-looking man, with a short, thin beard*] Mister, want to ask you ! Can they get blacklegs ?

BULGIN. [*Menacing*] Let 'em try.
                                    [*There are savage murmurs from the crowd.*
BROWN. [*A round-faced man*] Where could they get 'em then ?

EVANS. [*A small restless, harassed man, with a fighting face*] There's always blacklegs ; it's the nature of 'em. There's always men that'll save their own skins.
          [*Another savage murmur. There is a movement, and old THOMAS, joining the crowd, takes his stand in front.*

HARNESS. [*Holding up his hand*] They can't get them. But that won't help you. Now men, be reasonable. Your demands would have brought on us the burden of a dozen strikes at a time when we were not prepared for them. The Unions live by Justice, not to one, but all. Any fair man will tell you—you were ill-advised ! I don't say you go too far for that which you're entitled to, but you're going too far for the moment ; you've dug a pit for yourselves. Are you to stay there, or are you to climb out ? Come !

LEWIS. [*A clean-cut Welshman with a dark moustache*] You've hit it, Mister ! Which is it to be ?
          [*Another movement in the crowd, and ROUS, coming quickly, takes his stand next THOMAS.*

HARNESS. Cut your demands to the right pattern, and we'll see you through ; refuse, and don't expect me to waste my time coming down here again. I'm not the sort that speaks at random, as you ought to know by this time. If you're the sound men I take you for—no matter who advises you against it—[*he fixes his eyes on* ROBERTS] you'll make up your minds to come in, and trust to us to get your terms. Which is it to be ? Hands together, and victory—or—the starvation you've got now ?   [*A prolonged murmur from the crowd.*

JAGO. [*Sullenly*] Talk about what you know.

HARNESS. [*Lifting his voice above the murmur*] Know ? [*With cold passion.*] All that you've been through, my friend, I've been through —I was through it when I was no bigger than [*pointing to a youth*] that shaver there ; the Unions then weren't what they are now. What's made them strong ? It's hands together that's made them strong. I've been through it all, I tell you, the brand's on my soul yet. I know what you've suffered—there's nothing you can tell me that I don't know ; but the whole is greater than the part, and you are only the part. Stand by us, and we will stand by you.

> [*Quartering them with his eyes, he waits. The murmuring swells ; the men form little groups.* GREEN, BULGIN, *and* LEWIS *talk together.*

LEWIS. Speaks very sensible, the Union chap.

GREEN. [*Quietly*] Ah ! if I'd a been *listened* to, you'd 'ave 'eard sense these two months past.   [*The bargemen are seen laughing.*

LEWIS. [*Pointing*] Look at those two blanks over the fence there !

BULGIN. [*With gloomy violence*] They'd best stop their cackle, or I'll break their jaws.

JAGO. [*Suddenly*] You say the furnace men's paid enough ?

HARNESS. I did not say they were paid enough ; I said they were paid as much as the furnace men in similar works elsewhere.

EVANS. That's a lie. [*Hubbub.*] What about Harper's ?

HARNESS. [*With cold irony*] You may look at home for lies, my man. Harper's shifts are longer, the pay works out the same.

HENRY ROUS. [*A dark edition of his brother George*] Will ye support us in double pay overtime Saturdays ?

HARNESS. Yes, we will.

JAGO. What have ye done with our subscriptions ?

HARNESS. [*Coldly*] I have told you what we *will* do with them.

EVANS. Ah ! *will*, it's always will ! Ye'd have our mates desert us.   [*Hubbub.*

BULGIN. [*Shouting*] Hold your row !   [EVANS *looks round angrily.*

HARNESS. [*Lifting his voice*] Those who know their right hands from their lefts know that the Unions are neither thieves nor traitors. I've said my say. Figure it out, my lads ; when you want me you know where I shall be.

> [*He jumps down, the crowd gives way, he passes through them, and goes away. A bargeman looks after him, jerking his pipe with a derisive gesture. The men close up in groups, and many looks are cast at* ROBERTS, *who stands alone against the wall.*

EVANS. He wants ye to turn blacklegs, that's what he wants. He wants ye to go back on us. Sooner than turn blackleg—I'd starve, I would.

BULGIN. Who's talkin' o' blacklegs—mind what you're saying, will you ?

BLACKSMITH. [*A youth with yellow hair and huge arms*] What about the women ?

EVANS. They can stand what we can stand, I suppose, can't they ?

BLACKSMITH. Ye've no wife ?

EVANS. An' don't want one.

THOMAS. [*Raising his voice*] Aye ! Give us the power to come to terms with London, lads.

DAVIES. [*A dark, slow-fly, gloomy man*] Go up the platform, if you got anything to say, go up an' say it.

> [*There are cries of " Thomas ! " He is pushed towards the plat-
> form ; he ascends it with difficulty, and bares his head, waiting
> for silence.   A hush !*

RED-HAIRED YOUTH. [*Suddenly*] Coot old Thomas !

> [*A hoarse laugh ; the bargemen exchange remarks ; a hush again,
> and* THOMAS *begins speaking.*

THOMAS. We are all in the tepth together, and it iss Nature that has put us there.

HENRY ROUS. It's London put us there !

EVANS. It's the Union.

THOMAS. It iss not Lonton ; not it iss not the Union—it iss Nature. It iss no disgrace whateffer to a potty to give in to Nature.   For this Nature iss a fery pig thing ; it is pigger than what a man is.   There iss more years to my hett than to the hett of any one here.   It is fery pat, look you, this coing against Nature.   It is pat to make other potties suffer, when there is nothing to pe cot py it.

> [*A laugh.*   THOMAS *angrily goes on.*]

What are ye laughing at ?   It is pat, I say !   We are fighting for a principle ; there is nopotty that shall say I am not a peliever in principle.   Putt when Nature says " No further," then it is no coot snapping your fingers in her face.

> [*A laugh from* ROBERTS, *and murmurs of approval.*]

This Nature must pe humort.   It is a man's pisiness to pe pure, honest, just and merciful.   That's what Chapel tells you. [*To* ROBERTS, *angrily.*]   And, look you, David Roberts, Chapel tells you ye can do that without coing against Nature.

JAGO. What about the Union ?

THOMAS. I ton't trust the Union ; they haf treated us like tirt. " Do what we tell you," said they.   I haf peen captain of the furnace men twenty years, and I say to the Union—[*excitedly*]—" Can you tell me then, as well as I can tell you, what iss the right wages for the work that these men do ? "   For fife and twenty years I haf paid my moneys to the Union and—[*with great excitement*]—for nothings !   What iss that but roguery, for all that this Mr. Harness says !   [*Murmurs.*

EVANS. Hear, hear.

HENRY ROUS. Get on with you !   Cut on with it then !

THOMAS. Look you, if a man toes not trust me, am I coing to trust him ?

JAGO. That's right.

THOMAS. Let them alone for rogues, and act for ourselves.

> [*Murmurs.*

BLACKSMITH. That's what we been doin', haven't we ?

THOMAS. [*With increased excitement*] I wass brought up to do for

meself. I wass brought up to go without a thing, if I hat not moneys
to puy it. There iss too much, look you, of doing things with other
people's moneys. We haf fought fair, and if we haf peen beaten, it
iss no fault of ours. Gif us the power to make terms with London
for ourself ; if we ton't succeed, I say it iss petter to take our peating
like men, than to tie like togs, or hang on to others' coat-tails to make
them do our pusiness for us !

EVANS. [*Muttering*] Who wants to ?

THOMAS. [*Craning*] What's that ? If I stand up to a potty, and he
knocks me town, I am not to go hollering to other potties to help
me ; I am to stand up again ; and if he knocks me town properly, I
am to stay there, isn't that right ?   [*Laughter.*

JAGO. No Union !

HENRY ROUS. Union !   [*Others take up the shout.*

EVANS. Blacklegs !

        [BULGIN *and the* BLACKSMITH *shake their fists at* EVANS.

THOMAS. [*With a gesture*] I am an olt man, look you.

                [*A sudden silence, then murmurs again.*

LEWIS. Olt fool, with his " No Union ! "

BULGIN. Them furnace chaps ! For twopence I'd smash the faces
o' the lot of them.

GREEN. If I'd 'a been listened to at the first——

THOMAS. [*Wiping his brow*] I'm comin' now to what I was coing to
say——

DAVIES. [*Muttering*] An' time too !

THOMAS. [*Solemnly*] Chapel says : Ton't carry on this strike !
Put an end to it !

JAGO. That's a lie ! Chapel says go on !

THOMAS. [*Scornfully*] Inteet ! I haf ears to my head.

RED-HAIRED YOUTH. Ah ! long ones !   [*A laugh.*

JAGO. Your ears have misbeled you then.

THOMAS. [*Excitedly*] Ye cannot be right if I am, ye cannot haf it
both ways.

RED-HAIRED YOUTH. Chapel can though !

        [" *The Shaver* " *laughs ; there are murmurs from the crowd.*

THOMAS. [*Fixing his eyes on* " *The Shaver* "] Ah ! ye're coing
the roat to tamnation. An' so I say to all of you. If ye co
against Chapel I will not pe with you, nor will any other Got-fearing
man.

        [*He steps down from the patform.* JAGO *makes his way towards it.
        There are cries of* " *Don't let 'im go up !* "

JAGO. Don't let him go up ? That's free speech, that is. [*He
goes up.*] I ain't got much to say to you. Look at the matter plain ;
ye've come the road this far, and now you want to chuck the journey.
We've all been in one boat ; and now you want to pull in two. We

engineers have stood by you; ye're ready now, are ye, to give us the go-by? If we'd a-known that before, we'd not a-started out with you so early one bright morning! That's all I've got to say. Old man Thomas a'n't got his Bible lesson right. If you give up to London, or to Harness, now, it's givin' us the chuck— to save your skins—you won't get over that, my boys; it's a dirty thing to do.

> [*He gets down; during his little speech, which is ironically spoken, there is a restless discomfort in the crowd. ROUS, stepping forward, jumps on the platform. He has an air of fierce distraction. Sullen murmurs of disapproval from the crowd.*

ROUS. [*Speaking with great excitement*] I'm no blanky orator, mates, but wot I say is drove from me. What I say is yuman nature. Can a man set an' see 'is mother starve? Can 'e now?

ROBERTS. [*Starting forward*] Rous!

ROUS. [*Staring at him fiercely*] Sim 'Arness said fair! I've changed my mind.

EVANS. Ah! Turned your coat you mean!

> [*The crowd manifests a great surprise.*

LEWIS. [*Apostrophizing ROUS*] Hallo! What's turned him round?

ROUS. [*Speaking with intense excitement*] 'E said fair. "Stand by us," 'e said, "and we'll stand by you." That's where we've been makin' our mistake this long time past; and who's to blame for't? [*He points at ROBERTS.*] That man there! "No," 'e said, "fight the robbers," 'e said, "squeeze the breath out o' them!" But it's not the breath out o' them that's being squeezed; it's the breath out of *us* and *ours*, and that's the book of truth. I'm no orator, mates, it's the flesh and blood in me that's speakin', it's the heart o' me. [*With a menacing, yet half ashamed movement towards ROBERTS.*] He'll speak to you again, mark my words, but don't ye listen. [*The crowd groans.*] It's hell fire that's on that man's tongue. [ROBERTS *is seen laughing.*] Sim 'Arness is right. What are we without the Union— handful o' parched leaves—a puff o' smoke. I'm no orator, but I say: Chuck it up! Chuck it up! Sooner than go on starving the women and the children.

> [*The murmurs of acquiescence almost drown the murmurs of dissent.*

EVANS. What's turned *you* to blacklegging?

ROUS. [*With a furious look*] Sim 'Arness knows what he's talkin' about. Give us power to come to terms with London; I'm no orator, but I say—have done wi' this black misery!

> [*He gives his muffler a twist, jerks his head back and jumps off the platform. The crowd applauds and surges forward. Amid cries of "That's enough!" "Up Union!" "Up Harness!" ROBERTS quietly ascends the platform. There is a moment of silence.*

BLACKSMITH. We don't want to hear you.   Shut it !

HENRY ROUS. Get down !

> [*Amid such cries they surge towards the platform.*

EVANS. [*Fiercely*] Let 'im speak !   Roberts !   Roberts !

BULGIN. [*Muttering*] He'd better look out that I don't crack 'is skull.

> [ROBERTS *faces the crowd, probing them with his eyes till they gradually become silent. He begins speaking. One of the bargemen rises and stands.*

ROBERTS. You don't want to hear me, then ?   You'll listen to Rous and to that old man, but not to me.   You'll listen to Sim Harness of the Union that's treated you *so fair ;* maybe you'll listen to those men from London ?   Ah !   You groan !   What for ?   You love their feet on your necks, don't you ?   [*Then as* BULGIN *elbows his way towards the platform, with calm pathos.*] You'd like to break my jaw, John Bulgin.   Let me speak, then do your smashing, if it gives you pleasure.   [BULGIN *stands motionless and sullen.*] Am I a liar, a coward, a traitor ?   If only I were, ye'd listen to me, I'm sure.   [*The murmurings cease, and there is now dead silence.*] Is there a man of you here that has less to gain by striking ?   Is there a man of you that had more to lose ?   Is there a man of you that has given up *eight hundred* pounds since this trouble here began ?   Come now, is there ?   How much has Thomas given up—ten pounds or five, or what ?   You listened to him, and what had he to say ?   "None can pretend," he said, " that I'm not a believer in principle—[*with biting irony*]—but when Nature says :   ' No further, 'tes going agenst Nature.' "   *I* tell you if a man cannot say to Nature :   " Budge me from this if ye can ! "—[*with a sort of exaltation*]—his principles are but his belly. " Oh, but," Thomas says, " a man can be pure and honest, just and merciful, and take off his hat to Nature ! "   *I* tell you Nature's neither pure nor honest, just nor merciful.   You chaps that live over the hill, an' go home dead beat in the dark on a snowy night—don't ye fight your way every inch of it ?   Do ye go lyin' down an' trustin' to the tender mercies of this merciful Nature ?   Try it and you'll soon know with what ye've got to deal.   'Tes only by that—[*he strikes a blow with his clenched fist*]—in Nature's face that a man can be a man.   " Give in," says Thomas, " go down on your knees ; throw up your foolish fight, an' perhaps," he said, " perhaps your enemy will chuck you down a crust."

JAGO. Never !

EVANS. Curse them !

THOMAS. I nefer said that.

ROBERTS. [*Bitingly*] If ye did not say it, man, ye meant it.   An' what did ye say about Chapel ?   " Chapel's against it," ye said. " She's against it ! "   Well, if Chapel and Nature go hand in hand, it's the first I've ever heard of it.   That young man there—[*pointing to* ROUS]—said I 'ad 'ell fire on my tongue.   If I had I would use it all to scorch and wither this talking of surrender.   Surrendering's the work of cowards and traitors.

HENRY ROUS. [*As* GEORGE ROUS *moves forward*] Go for him, George—don't stand his lip !

ROBERTS. [*Flinging out his finger*] Stop there, George Rous, it's no time this to settle personal matters.   [ROUS *stops*.] But there was one other spoke to you—Mr. Simon Harness.   We have not much to thank Mr. Harness and the Union for.   They said to us " Desert your mates, or we'll desert you."   An' they did desert us.

EVANS. They did.

ROBERTS. Mr. Simon Harness is a clever man, but he has come too late.   [*With intense conviction*.] For all that Mr. Simon Harness says, for all that Thomas, Rous, for all that any man present here can say— *We've won the fight !*

[*The crowd sags nearer, looking eagerly up.   With withering scorn*.] You've felt the pinch o't in your bellies.   You've forgotten what that fight 'as been ; many times I have told you ; I will tell you now this once again.   The fight o' the country's body and blood against a blood-sucker.   The fight of those that spend theirselves with every blow they strike and every breath they draw, against a thing that fattens on them, and grows and grows by the law of *merciful* Nature. That thing is Capital !   A thing that buys the sweat o' men's brows, and the tortures o' their brains, at its own price.   *Don't I* know that ? Wasn' the work o' *my* brains bought for seven hundred pounds, and hasn't one hundred thousand pounds been gained them by that seven hundred without the stirring of a finger ?   It is a thing that will take as much and give you as little as it can.   That's *Capital !*   A thing that will say—" I'm very sorry for you, poor fellows—you have a cruel time of it, I know," but will not give one sixpence of its dividends to help you have a better time.   That's Capital !   Tell me, for all their talk is there one of them that will consent to another penny on the Income Tax to help the poor ?   That's Capital !   A white-faced, stony-hearted monster !   Ye have got it on its knees ; are ye to give up at the last minute to save your miserable bodies pain ?   When I went this morning to those old men from London, I looked into their very 'earts.   One of them was sitting there—Mr. Scantlebury, a mass of flesh nourished on us : sittin' there for all the world like the shareholders in this Company, that sit not moving tongue nor finger, takin' dividends—a great dumb ox that can only be roused when its food is threatened.   I looked into his eyes and I saw *he was afraid*—afraid for himself and his dividends, afraid for his fees, afraid of the very shareholders he stands for ; and all but one of them's afraid—like children that get into a wood at night, and start at every rustle of the leaves. I ask you, men—[*he pauses, holding out his hand till there is utter silence*]—Give me a free hand to tell them : " Go you back to London. The men have nothing for you ! " [*A murmuring.*] Give me that, an' I swear to you, within a week you shall have from London all you want.

EVANS, JAGO, AND OTHERS. A free hand !   Give him a free hand ! Bravo—bravo !

ROBERTS. 'Tis not for this little moment of time we're fighting [*the murmuring dies*], not for ourselves, our own little bodies, and their wants, 'tis for all those that come after throughout all time. [*With intense sadness.*] Oh ! men—for the love o' them, don't roll up another stone upon their heads, don't help to blacken the sky, an' let the bitter sea in over them. They're welcome to the worst that can happen to me, to the worst that can happen to us all, aren't they—aren't they ? If we can shake [*passionately*] that white-faced monster with the bloody lips, that has sucked the life out of ourselves, our wives and children, since the world began. [*Dropping the note of passion, but with the utmost weight and intensity.*] If we have not the hearts of men to stand against it breast to breast, and eye to eye, and force it backward till it cry for mercy, it will go on sucking life ; and we shall stay for ever what we are [*in almost a whisper*] less than the very dogs.

[*An utter stillness, and* ROBERTS *stands rocking his body slightly, with his eyes burning the faces of the crowd.*

EVANS AND JAGO. [*Suddenly*] Roberts !   [*The shout is taken up.*]
        [*There is a slight movement in the crowd, and* MADGE *passing below the towing-path stops by the platform, looking up at* ROBERTS. *A sudden doubting silence.*

ROBERTS. " Nature," says that old man, " give in to Nature." *I* tell you, strike your blow in Nature's face — an' let it do its worst !

        [*He catches sight of* MADGE, *his brows contract, he looks away.*

MADGE. [*In a low voice—close to the platform*] Your wife's dying !

        [ROBERTS *glares at her as if torn from some pinnacle of exaltation.*

ROBERTS. [*Trying to stammer on*] I say to you—answer them—answer them——   [*He is drowned by the murmur in the crowd.*

THOMAS. [*Stepping forward*] Ton't you hear her, then ?

ROBERTS. What is it ?   [*A dead silence.*

THOMAS. Your wife, man !

        [ROBERTS *hesitates, then with a gesture, he leaps down, and goes away below the towing-path, the men making way for him. The standing bargeman opens and prepares to light a lantern. Daylight is fast failing.*

MADGE. He needn't have hurried ! Annie Roberts is dead. [*Then *in the silence, passionately.*] You pack of blinded hounds ! How many more women are you going to let die ?

> [*The crowd shrinks back from her, and breaks up in groups, with a confused, uneasy movement.* MADGE *goes quickly away below the towing-path. There is a hush as they look after her.*

LEWIS. There's a spitfire, for ye !

BULGIN. [*Growling*] I'll smash 'er jaw.

GREEN. If I'd a-been listened to, that poor woman——

THOMAS. It's a judgment on him for coing against Chapel. I toit him how 'twould be !

EVANS. All the more reason for sticking by 'im. [*A cheer.*] Are you goin' to desert him now 'e's down ? Are you goin' to chuck him over, now 'e's lost 'is wife ?

> [*The crowd is murmuring and cheering all at once.*

ROUS. [*Stepping in front of platform*] Lost his wife ! Aye ! Can't ye see ? Look at home, look at your own wives ! What's to save them ? Ye'll have the same in all your houses before long !

LEWIS. Aye, aye !

HENRY ROUS. Right ! George, right !

> [*There are murmurs of assent.*

ROUS. It's not us that's blind, it's Roberts. How long will ye put up with 'im !

HENRY ROUS, BULGIN, DAVIES. Give 'im the chuck !

> [*The cry is taken up.*

EVANS. [*Fiercely*] Kick a man that's down ? Down ?

HENRY ROUS. Stop his jaw there !

> [EVANS *throws up his arm at a threat from* BULGIN. *The barge-man, who has lighted the lantern, holds it high above his head.*

ROUS. [*Springing on to the platform*] What brought him down then, but 'is own black obstinacy ? Are ye goin' to follow a man that can't see better than that where he's goin' ?

EVANS. He's lost 'is wife.

ROUS. An' who's fault's that but his own ? 'Ave done with 'im, I say, before he's killed your own wives and mothers.

DAVIES. Down im !

HENRY ROUS. He's finished !

BROWN. We've had enough of 'im !

BLACKSMITH. Too much !

> [*The crowd takes up these cries, excepting only* EVANS, JAGO, *and* GREEN, *who is seen to argue mildly with the* BLACKSMITH.

ROUS. [*Above the hubbub*] We'll make terms with the Union, lads.

> [*Cheers.*

EVANS. [*Fiercely*] Ye blacklegs !

BULGIN. [*Savagely—squaring up to him*] Who are ye callin' black-legs, Rat?

> [EVANS *throws up his fists, parries the blow, and returns it. They fight. The bargemen are seen holding up the lantern and enjoying the sight. Old* THOMAS *steps forward and holds out his hands.*

THOMAS. Shame on your strife!

> [*The* BLACKSMITH, BROWN, LEWIS, *and the* RED-HAIRED YOUTH *pull* EVANS *and* BULGIN *apart. The stage is almost dark.*

The curtain falls.

ACT III

It is five o'clock. In the UNDERWOOD'S *drawing-room, which is artistically furnished,* ENID *is sitting on the sofa working at a baby's frock.* EDGAR, *by a little spindle-legged table in the centre of the room, is fingering a china-box. His eyes are fixed on the double doors that lead into the dining-room.*

EDGAR. [*Putting down the china-box, and glancing at his watch*] Just on five, they're all in there waiting, except Frank. Where's he?

ENID. He's had to go down to Gasgoyne's about a contract. Will you want him?

EDGAR. He can't help us. This is a directors' job. [*Motioning towards a single door half hidden by a curtain.*] Father in his room?

ENID. Yes.

EDGAR. I wish he'd stay there, Enid.   [ENID *looks up at him.*] This is a beastly business, old girl?

[*He takes up the little box again and turns it over and over.*]

ENID. I went to the Roberts's this afternoon, Ted.

EDGAR. That wasn't very wise.

ENID. He's simply killing his wife.

EDGAR. We are, you mean.

ENID. [*Suddenly*] Roberts ought to give way!

EDGAR. There's a lot to be said on the men's side.

ENID. I don't feel half so sympathetic with them as I did before I went. They just set up class feeling against you. Poor Annie was looking dreadfully bad—fire going out, and nothing fit for her to eat.   [EDGAR *walks to and fro.*] But she would stand up for Roberts. When you see all this wretchedness going on and feel you can do nothing, you have to shut your eyes to the whole thing.

EDGAR. If you can.

ENID. When I went I was all on their side, but as soon as I got there I began to feel quite different at once. People talk about sympathy with the working classes, they don't know what it means to try and put it into practice. It seems hopeless.

EDGAR. Ah! well.

ENID. It's dreadful going on with the men in this state. I do hope the Dad will make concessions.

EDGAR. He won't. [*Gloomily.*] It's a sort of religion with him. Curse it! I know what's coming! He'll be voted down.

ENID. They wouldn't dare !

EDGAR. They will—they're in a funk.

ENID. [*Indignantly*] He'd never stand it !

EDGAR. [*With a shrug*] My dear girl, if you're beaten in a vote, you've got to stand it.

ENID. Oh ! [*She gets up in alarm.*] But would he resign ?

EDGAR. Of course ! It goes to the roots of his beliefs.

ENID. But he's so *wrapped up in this company*, Ted ! There'd be nothing left for him ! It'd be dreadful !

[EDGAR *shrugs his shoulders.*]

Oh, Ted, he's so old now ! You mustn't let them !

EDGAR. [*Hiding his feelings in an outburst*] My sympathies in this strike are all on the side of the men.

ENID. He's been Chairman for more than thirty years ! He made the whole thing ! And think of the bad times they've had, it's always been he who pulled them through. Oh, Ted, you must——

EDGAR. What is it you want ? You said just now you hoped he'd make concessions. Now you want me to back him in not making them. This isn't a game, Enid !

ENID. [*Hotly*] It isn't a game to *me* that the Dad's in danger of losing all he cares about in life. If he won't give way, and he's beaten, it'll simply break him down !

EDGAR. Didn't you say it was dreadful going on with the men in this state ?

ENID. But can't you see, Ted, Father'll never get over it ! You must stop them somehow. The others are afraid of him. If you back him up——

EDGAR. [*Putting his hand to his head*] Against my convictions— against yours ! The moment it begins to pinch one personally——

ENID. It isn't personal, it's the Dad !

EDGAR. Your family or yourself, and over goes the show !

ENID. [*Resentfully*] If you don't take it seriously, I do.

EDGAR. I am as fond of him as you are ; that's nothing to do with it.

ENID. We can't tell about the men ; it's all guess-work. But we know the Dad might have a stroke any day. D'you mean to say that he isn't more to you than——

EDGAR. Of course he is.

ENID. I don't understand you then.

EDGAR. H'm !

ENID. If it were for oneself it would be different, but for our own Father ! You don't seem to realize.

EDGAR. I realize perfectly.

ENID. It's your first duty to save him.

EDGAR. I wonder.

ENID. [*Imploring*] Oh, Ted! It's the only interest he's got left; it'll be like a death-blow to him!

EDGAR. [*Restraining his emotion*] I know.

ENID. Promise!

EDGAR. I'll do what I can. [*He turns to the double doors.*

> [*The curtained door is opened, and* ANTHONY *appears.* EDGAR *opens the double doors, and passes through.*
>
> [SCANTLEBURY'S *voice is faintly heard:* "*Past five; we shall never get through—have to eat another dinner at that hotel!*" *The doors are shut.* ANTHONY *walks forward.*

ANTHONY. You've been seeing Roberts, I hear.

ENID. Yes.

ANTHONY. Do you know what trying to bridge such a gulf as this is like? [ENID *puts her work on the little table, and faces him.*] Filling a sieve with sand!

ENID. Don't!

ANTHONY. You think with your gloved hands you can cure the trouble of the century. [*He passes on.*

ENID. Father! [ANTHONY *stops at the double doors.*] I'm only thinking of you!

ANTHONY. [*More softly*] I can take care of myself, my dear.

ENID. Have you thought what'll happen if you're beaten—[*she points*]—in there?

ANTHONY. I don't mean to be.

ENID. Oh! Father, don't give them a chance. You're not well; need you go to the meeting at all?

ANTHONY. [*With a grim smile*] Cut and run?

ENID. But they'll outvote you!

ANTHONY. [*Putting his hand on the doors*] We shall see!

ENID. I beg you, Dad! [ANTHONY *looks at her softly.*] Won't you?

> [ANTHONY *shakes his head. He opens the doors. A buzz of voices comes in.*

SCANTLEBURY. Can one get dinner on that 6.30 train up?

TENCH. No, sir, I believe not, sir.

WILDER. Well, I shall speak out; I've had enough of this.

EDGAR. [*Sharply*] What?

> [*It ceases instantly.* ANTHONY *passes through, closing the doors behind him.* ENID *springs to them with a gesture of dismay. She puts her hand on the knob, and begins turning it; then goes to the fireplace, and taps her foot on the fender. Suddenly she rings the bell.* FROST *comes in by the door that leads into the hall.*

FROST. Yes, M'm?

ENID. When the men come, Frost, please show them in here; the hall's cold.

FROST. I could put them in the pantry, M'm.

ENID. No. I don't want to—to offend them; they're so touchy.

FROST. Yes, M'm. [*Pause.*] Excuse me, Mr. Anthony's 'ad nothing to eat all day.

ENID. I know, Frost.

FROST. Nothin' but two whiskies and sodas, M'm.

ENID. Oh! you oughtn't to have let him have those.

FROST. [*Gravely*] Mr. Anthony is a little difficult, M'm. It's not as if he were a younger man, an' knew what was good for 'im; he will have his own way.

ENID. I suppose we all want that.

FROST. Yes, M'm. [*Quietly.*] Excuse me speakin' about the strike. I'm sure if the other gentlemen were to give up to Mr. Anthony, and quietly let the men 'ave what they want, afterwards, that'd be the best way. I find that very useful with him at times, M'm.

[ENID *shakes her head.*]

If he's crossed, it makes him violent [*with an air of discovery*], and I've noticed in my own case, when I'm violent I'm always sorry for it afterwards.

ENID. [*With a smile*] Are *you* ever violent, Frost?

FROST. Yes, M'm; oh! sometimes very violent.

ENID. I've never seen you.

FROST. [*Impersonally*] No, M'm; that is so.

[ENID *fidgets towards the door's back.*]

[*With feeling.*] Bein' with Mr. Anthony, as you know, M'm, ever since I was fifteen, it worries me to see him crossed like this at his age. I've taken the liberty to speak to Mr. Wanklin [*dropping his voice*]—seems to be the most sensible of the gentlemen—but 'e said to me: " That's all very well, Frost, but this strike's a very serious thing," 'e said. " Serious for all parties, no doubt," I said, " but yumour 'im, sir," I said, " yumour 'im. It's like this, if a man comes to a stone wall, 'e doesn't drive 'is 'ead against it, 'e gets over it." " Yes," 'e said, " you'd better tell your master that." [FROST *looks at his nails.*] That's where it is, M'm. I said to Mr. Anthony this morning: " Is it worth it, sir?" " Damn it," he said to me, " Frost! Mind your own business, or take a month's notice!" Beg pardon, M'm, for using such a word.

ENID. [*Moving to the double doors, and listening*] Do you know that man Roberts, Frost?

FROST. Yes, M'm; that's to say, not to speak to. But to *look* at 'im you can tell what *he's* like.

ENID. [*Stopping*] Yes?

FROST. He's not one of these 'ere ordinary 'armless Socialists. 'E's violent; got a fire inside 'im. What I call " personal." A man may 'ave what opinion 'e likes, so long as 'e's not personal; when 'e's that 'e's *not* safe.

ENID. I think that's what my Father feels about Roberts.

FROST. No doubt, M'm, Mr. Anthony has a feeling against him.

> [ENID *glances at him sharply, but finding him in perfect earnest, stands biting her lips, and looking at the double doors.*]

It's a regular right down struggle between the two. I've no patience with this Roberts, from what I 'ear he's just an ordinary workin' man like the rest of 'em. If he did invent a thing he's no worse off than 'undreds of others. My brother invented a new kind o' dumb waiter—nobody gave *him* anything for it, an' there it is, bein' used all over the place. [ENID *moves closer to the double doors.*] There's a kind o' man that never forgives the world, because 'e wasn't born a gentleman. What I say is—no man that's a gentleman looks down on another man because 'e 'appens to be a class or two above 'im, no more than if 'e 'appens to be a class or two below.

ENID. [*With slight impatience*] Yes, I know, Frost, of course. Will you please go in and ask if they'll have some tea; say I sent you.

FROST. Yes, M'm.

> [*He opens the doors gently and goes in. There is a momentary sound of earnest, rather angry talk.*]

WILDER. I don't agree with you.

WANKLIN. We've had this over a dozen times.

EDGAR. [*Impatiently*] Well, what's the proposition?

SCANTLEBURY. Yes, what does your Father say? Tea? Not for me, not for me!

WANKLIN. What I understand the Chairman to say is this——

> [FROST *re-enters, closing the door behind him.*

ENID. [*Moving from the door*] Won't they have any tea, Frost?

> [*She goes to the little table, and remains motionless, looking at the baby's frock.*   [*A parlourmaid enters from the hall.*

PARLOURMAID. A Miss Thomas, M'm.

ENID. [*Raising her head*] Thomas? What Miss Thomas—d'you mean a—— ?

PARLOURMAID. Yes, M'm.

ENID. [*Blankly*] Oh! Where is she?

PARLOURMAID. In the porch.

ENID. I don't want—— [*She hesitates.*]

FROST. Shall I dispose of her, M'm?

ENID. I'll come out. No, show her in here, Ellen.

> [*The PARLOURMAID and FROST go out. ENID pursing her lips, sits at the little table, taking up the baby's frock. The PARLOURMAID ushers in MADGE THOMAS and goes out; MADGE stands by the door.*

ENID. Come in. What is it? What have you come for, please?

MADGE. Brought a message from Mrs. Roberts.

ENID. A message ?   Yes.

MADGE. She asks you to look after her Mother.

ENID. I don't understand.

MADGE. [*Sullenly*] That's the message.

ENID. But—what—why ?

MADGE. Annie Roberts is dead.   [*There is a silence.*

ENID. [*Horrified*] But it's only a little more than an hour since I saw her.

MADGE. Of cold and hunger.

ENID. [*Rising*] Oh ! that's not true ! the poor thing's heart——
What makes you look at me like that ?   I tried to help her.

MADGE. [*With suppressed savagery*] I thought you'd like to know.

ENID. [*Passionately*] It's so unjust !   Can't you see that I want to help you all ?

MADGE. I never harmed anyone that hadn't harmed me first.

ENID. [*Coldly*] What harm have I done you ?   Why do you speak to me like that ?

MADGE. [*With the bitterest intensity*] You come out of your comfort to spy on us !   A week of hunger, that's what *you* want !

ENID. [*Standing her ground*] Don't talk nonsense !

MADGE. I saw her die ; her hands were blue with the cold.

ENID. [*With a movement of grief*] Oh ! why wouldn't she let me help her ?   It's such senseless pride !

MADGE. Pride's better than nothing to keep your body warm.

ENID. [*Passionately*] I won't talk to you !   How can you tell what I feel ?   It's not my fault that I was born better off than you.

MADGE. We don't want your money.

ENID. You don't understand, and you don't want to ; please to go away !

MADGE. [*Balefully*] You've killed her, for all your soft words, you and your father——

ENID. [*With rage and emotion*] That's wicked !   My father is suffering himself through this wretched strike.

MADGE. [*With sombre triumph*] Then tell him Mrs. Roberts is dead ! That'll make him better.

ENID. Go away !

MADGE. When a person hurts us we get it back on them.

> [*She makes a sudden and swift movement towards* ENID, *fixing her eyes on the child's frock lying across the little table.* ENID *snatches the frock up, as though it were the child itself. They stand a yard apart, crossing glances.*

MADGE. [*Pointing to the frock with a little smile*] Ah !   You felt *that* !   Lucky it's her mother—not her children—you've to look after, isn't it.   *She* won't trouble you long !

ENID. Go away!

MADGE. I've given you the message.

> [*She turns and goes out into the hall.* ENID, *motionless till she has gone, sinks down at the table, bending her head over the frock, which she is still clutching to her. The double doors are opened, and* ANTHONY *comes slowly in; he passes his daughter, and lowers himself into an arm-chair. He is very flushed.*

ENID. [*Hiding her emotion—anxiously*] What is it, Dad? ANTHONY *makes a gesture, but does not speak.*] Who was it?

> [ANTHONY *does not answer.* ENID *going to the double doors meets* EDGAR *coming in. They speak together in low tones.*]

What is it, Ted?

EDGAR. That fellow Wilder! Taken to personalities! He was downright insulting.

ENID. What did he *say*?

EDGAR. Said, Father was too old and feeble to know what he was doing! The Dad's worth six of him!

ENID. Of course he is.   [*They look at* ANTHONY.

> [*The doors open wider,* WANKLIN *appears with* SCANTLEBURY.

SCANTLEBURY. [*Sotto voce*] I don't like the look of this!

WANKLIN. [*Going forward*] Come, Chairman! Wilder sends you his apologies. A man can't do more.

> [WILDER, *followed by* TENCH, *comes in, and goes to* ANTHONY.

WILDER. [*Glumly*] I withdraw my words, sir. I'm sorry.

> [ANTHONY *nods to him.*

ENID. You haven't come to a decision, Mr. Wanklin?

> [WANKLIN *shakes his head.*

WANKLIN. We're all here, Chairman; what do you say? Shall we get on with the business, or shall we go back to the other room?

SCANTLEBURY. Yes, yes; let's get on. We must settle something.

> [*He turns from a small chair, and settles himself suddenly in the largest chair, with a sigh of comfort.*

> [WILDER *and* WANKLIN *also sit; and* TENCH, *drawing up a straight-backed chair close to his Chairman, sits on the edge of it with the minute-book and a stylographic pen.*

ENID. [*Whispering*] I want to speak to you a minute, Ted.

> [*They go out through the double doors.*

WANKLIN. Really, Chairman, it's no use soothing ourselves with a sense of false security. If this strike's not brought to an end before the General Meeting, the shareholders will certainly haul us over the coals.

SCANTLEBURY. [*Stirring*] What—what's that?

WANKLIN. I know it for a fact.

ANTHONY. Let them!

WILDER. And get turned out?

WANKLIN. [*To* ANTHONY] I don't mind martyrdom for a policy in which I believe, but I object to being burnt for someone else's principles.

SCANTLEBURY. Very reasonable—you must see that, Chairman.

ANTHONY. We owe it to other employers to stand firm.

WANKLIN. There's a limit to that.

ANTHONY. You were all full of fight at the start.

SCANTLEBURY. [*With a sort of groan*] We thought the men would give in, but they—haven't!

ANTHONY. They will!

WILDER. [*Rising and pacing up and down*] I can't have my reputation as a man of business destroyed for the satisfaction of starving the men out. [*Almost in tears.*] I can't have it! How can we meet the shareholders with things in the state they are?

SCANTLEBURY. Hear, hear—hear, hear!

WILDER. [*Lashing himself*] If anyone expects me to say to them I've lost you fifty thousand pounds and sooner than put my pride in my pocket I'll lose you another—— [*Glancing at* ANTHONY.] It's —it's unnatural! *I don't want to* go against you, sir——

WANKLIN. [*Persuasively*] Come, Chairman, we're *not* free agents. We're part of a machine. Our only business is to see the Company earns as much profit as it safely can. If you blame me for want of principle: I say that we're Trustees. Reason tells us we shall never get back in the saving of wages what we shall lose if we continue this struggle—really, Chairman, we *must* bring it to an end, on the best terms we can make.

ANTHONY. No!   [*There is a pause of general dismay.*

WILDER. It's a deadlock then. [*Letting his hands drop with a sort of despair.*] Now I shall never get off to Spain!

WANKLIN. [*Retaining a trace of irony*] You hear the consequences of your victory, Chairman?

WILDER. [*With a burst of feeling*] My wife's *ill!*

SCANTLEBURY. Dear, dear! You don't say so!

WILDER. If I don't get her out of this cold, I won't answer for the consequences.

          [*Through the double doors* EDGAR *comes in looking very grave.*

EDGAR. [*To his Father*] Have you heard this, sir? Mrs. Roberts is dead!

          [*Everyone stares at him, as if trying to gauge the importance of this news.*

Enid saw her this afternoon, she had no coals, or food, or anything. It's enough!

          [*There is a silence, everyone avoiding the other's eyes, except* ANTHONY, *who stares hard at his son.*

SCANTLEBURY. You don't suggest that we could have helped the poor thing ?

WILDER. [*Flustered*] The woman was in bad health. Nobody can say there's any responsibility on us. At least—not on me.

EDGAR. [*Hotly*] I say that we *are* responsible.

ANTHONY. War is war !

EDGAR. Not on women !

WANKLIN. It not infrequently happens that women are the greatest sufferers.

EDGAR. If we knew that, all the more responsibility rests on us.

ANTHONY. This is no matter for amateurs.

EDGAR. Call me what you like, sir. It's sickened me. We had no right to carry things to such a length.

WILDER. I don't like this business a bit—that Radical rag will twist it to their own ends ; see if they don't ! They'll get up some cock-and-bull story about the poor woman's dying from starvation. I wash my hands of it.

EDGAR. You can't. None of us can.

SCANTLEBURY. [*Striking his fist on the arm of his chair*] But I protest against this——

EDGAR. Protest as you like, Mr. Scantlebury, it won't alter facts.

ANTHONY. That's enough.

EDGAR. [*Facing him angrily*] No, sir. I tell you exactly what I think. If we pretend the men are not suffering, it's humbug ; and if they're suffering, we know enough of human nature to know the women are suffering more, and as to the children—well—it's damnable !   [SCANTLEBURY *rises from his chair.*] I don't say that we meant to be cruel, I don't say anything of the sort ; but I do say it's criminal to shut our eyes to the facts. We employ these men, and we can't get out of it. I don't care so much about the men, but I'd sooner resign my position on the Board than go on starving women in this way.

[*All except* ANTHONY *are now upon their feet*, ANTHONY *sits grasping the arms of his chair and staring at his son.*

SCANTLEBURY. I don't—I don't like the way you're putting it, young sir.

WANKLIN. You're rather overshooting the mark.

WILDER. I should think so indeed !

EDGAR. [*Losing control*] It's no use blinking things ! if *you* want to have the death of women on your hands—*I* don't !

SCANTLEBURY. Now, now, young man !

WILDER. On *our* hands ? Not on *mine*, I won't have it !

EDGAR. We are five members of this Board ; if we were four against it, why did we let it drift till it came to this ? You know perfectly well why—because we hoped we should starve the men out. Well, all we've done is to starve one woman out!

SCANTLEBURY. [*Almost hysterically*] I protest, I protest! I'm a humane man—we're all humane men!

EDGAR. [*Scornfully*] There's nothing wrong with our *humanity*. It's our imaginations, Mr. Scantlebury.

WILDER. Nonsense! My imagination's as good as yours.

EDGAR. If so, it isn't good enough.

WILDER. I foresaw this!

EDGAR. Then why didn't you put your foot down!

WILDER. Much good that would have done.

[*He looks at* ANTHONY.

EDGAR. If you, and I, and each one of us here who say that our imaginations are so good——

SCANTLEBURY. [*Flurried*] I never said so.

EDGAR. [*Paying no attention*] ——had put our feet down, the thing would have been ended long ago, and this poor woman's life wouldn't have been crushed out of her like this. For all we can tell there may be a dozen other starving women.

SCANTLEBURY. For God's sake, sir, don't use that word at a—at a Board meeting; it's—it's monstrous.

EDGAR. I *will* use it, Mr. Scantlebury.

SCANTLEBURY. Then I shall not listen to you. I shall not listen! It's painful to me. [*He covers his ears.*

WANKLIN. None of us are opposed to a settlement, except your Father.

EDGAR. I'm certain that if the shareholders knew——

WANKLIN. I don't think you'll find their imaginations are any better than ours. Because a woman happens to have a weak heart——

EDGAR. A struggle like this finds out the weak spots in everybody. Any child knows that. If it hadn't been for this cut-throat policy, she needn't have died like this; and there wouldn't be all this misery that anyone who isn't a fool can see is going on.

[*Throughout the foregoing* ANTHONY *has eyed his son; he now moves as though to rise, but stops as* EDGAR *speaks again.*]

I don't defend the men, or myself, or anybody.

WANKLIN. You may have to! A coroner's jury of disinterested sympathizers may say some very nasty things. We mustn't lose sight of our position.

SCANTLEBURY. [*Without uncovering his ears*] Coroner's jury! No, no, it's not a case for that?

EDGAR. I've had enough of cowardice.

WANKLIN. Cowardice is an unpleasant word, Mr. Edgar Anthony. It will look very like cowardice if we suddenly concede the men's demands when a thing like this happens; we must be careful!

WILDER. Of course we must. We've no knowledge of this matter, except a rumour. The proper course is to put the whole thing into the hands of Harness to settle for us ; that's natural, that's what we *should* have come to any way.

SCANTLEBURY. [*With dignity*] Exactly ! [*Turning to* EDGAR.] And as to you, young sir, I can't sufficiently express my—my distaste for the way you've treated the whole matter. You ought to withdraw ! Talking of starvation, talking of cowardice ! Considering what our views are ! Except your own Father—we're all agreed the only policy is—is one of goodwill—it's most irregular, it's most improper, and all I can say is it's—it's given me pain——

> [*He places his hand on the centre of his scheme.*

EDGAR. [*Stubbornly*] I withdraw nothing.

> [*He is about to say more when* SCANTLEBURY *once more covers up his ears.* TENCH *suddenly makes a demonstration with the minute-book. A sense of having been engaged in the unusual comes over all of them, and one by one they resume their seats.* EDGAR *alone remains on his feet.*

WILDER. [*With an air of trying to wipe something out*] I pay no attention to what young Mr. Anthony has said. Coroner's Jury ! The idea's preposterous. I—I move this amendment to the Chairman's Motion : That the dispute be placed at once in the hands of Mr. Simon Harness for settlement, on the lines indicated by him this morning. Anyone second that ?   [TENCH *writes in the book.*

WANKLIN. I do.

WILDER. Very well, then ; I ask the Chairman to put it to the Board.

ANTHONY. [*With a great sigh—slowly*] We have been made the subject of an attack. [*Looking round at* WILDER *and* SCANTLEBURY *with ironical contempt.*] I take it on *my* shoulders. I am seventy-six years old. I have been Chairman of this Company since its inception two-and-thirty years ago. I have seen it pass through good and evil report. My connection with it began in the year that this young man was born.

> [EDGAR *bows his head.* ANTHONY, *gripping his chair, goes on.*

I have had to do with " men " for fifty years ; I've always stood up to them ; I have never been beaten yet. I have fought the men of this Company four times, and four times I have beaten them. It has been said that I am not the man I was. [*He looks at* WILDER.] However that may be, I am man enough to stand to my guns.

> [*His voice grows stronger. The double doors are opened.* ENID *slips in, followed by* UNDERWOOD, *who restrains her.*

The men have been treated justly, they have had fair wages, we have always been ready to listen to complaints. It has been said that times have changed ; if they have, I have not changed with them.

Neither will I. It has been said that masters and men are equal !
Cant ! There can only be one master in a house ! Where two men
meet the better man will rule. It has been said that Capital and
Labour have the same interests. Cant ! Their interests are as wide
asunder as the poles. It has been said that the Board is only part of
a machine. Cant ! We *are* the machine ; its brains and sinews ;
it is for us to lead and to determine what is to be done, and to do it
without fear or favour. Fear of the men ! Fear of the shareholders !
Fear of our own shadows ! Before I am like that, I hope to die.

[*He pauses, and meeting his son's eyes, goes on.*]
There is only one way of treating " men "—with *the iron hand.* This
half-and-half business, the half-and-half manners of this generation
has brought all this upon us. Sentiment and softness, and what this
young man, no doubt, would call his social policy. You can't eat
cake and have it ! This middle-class sentiment, or socialism, or
whatever it may be, is rotten. Masters are masters, men are men !
Yield one demand, and they will make it six. They are [*he smiles
grimly*] like Oliver Twist, asking for more. If I were in *their* place
I should be the same. But I am not in their place. Mark my words :
one fine morning, when you have given way here, and given way
there—you will find you have parted with the ground beneath your
feet, and are deep in the bog of bankruptcy ; and with you, floundering
in that bog, will be the very men you have given way to. I have been
accused of being a domineering tyrant, thinking only of my pride—
I am thinking of the future of this country, threatened with the black
waters of confusion, threatened with mob government, threatened
with what I cannot see. If by any conduct of mine I help to
bring this on us, I shall be ashamed to look my fellows in the
face.

[ANTHONY *stares before him, at what he cannot see, and there is
        perfect stillness.* FROST *comes in from the hall, and all but
        ANTHONY look round at him uneasily.*
FROST. [*To his master*] The men are here, sir.

[ANTHONY *makes a gesture of dismissal.*]
Shall I bring them in, sir ?
ANTHONY. Wait !

[FROST *goes out,* ANTHONY *turns to face his son.*]
I come to the attack that has been made upon me.

[EDGAR, *with a gesture of deprecation, remains motionless with his
        head a little bowed.*]
A woman has died. I am told that her blood is on my hands ; I
am told that on my hands is the starvation and the suffering of other
women and of children.
EDGAR. I said " on *our* hands," sir.
ANTHONY. It is the same. [*His voice grows stronger and stronger,*

his feeling is more and more made manifest.] I am not aware that if my adversary suffer in a fair fight not sought by me, it is *my* fault. If I fall under *his* feet—as fall I may—I shall not complain. That will be *my* look-out—and this is—his. I cannot separate, as I would, these men from their women and children. A fair fight is a fair fight ! Let them learn to think before they pick a quarrel !

EDGAR. [*In a low voice*] But is it a fair fight, Father ? Look at them, and look at us ! They've only this one weapon !

ANTHONY. [*Grimly*] And you're weak-kneed enough to teach them how to use it ! It seems the fashion nowadays for men to take their enemy's side. I have not learnt that art. Is it my fault that they quarrelled with their Union too ?

EDGAR. There is such a thing as Mercy.

ANTHONY. And Justice comes before it.

EDGAR. What seems just to one man, sir, is injustice to another.

ANTHONY. [*With suppressed passion*] You accuse me of injustice —of what amounts to inhumanity—of cruelty——

[EDGAR *makes a gesture of horror—a general frightened movement.*

WANKLIN. Come, come, Chairman !

ANTHONY. [*In a grim voice*] These are the words of my own son. They are the words of a generation that I don't understand ; the words of a soft breed.

[*A general murmur. With a violent effort* ANTHONY *recovers his control.*

EDGAR. [*Quietly*] I said it of *myself*, too, Father.

[*A long look is exchanged between them, and* ANTHONY *puts out his hand with a gesture as if to sweep the personalities away ; then places it against his brow, swaying as though from giddiness. There is a movement towards him. He waves them back.*

ANTHONY. Before I put this amendment to the Board, I have one more word to say. [*He looks from face to face.*] If it is carried, it means that we shall fail in what we set ourselves to do. It means that we shall fail in the duty that we owe to all Capital. It means that we shall fail in the duty that we owe ourselves. It means that we shall be open to constant attack to which we as constantly shall have to yield. Be under no misapprehension—run this time, and you will never make a stand again ! You will have to fly like curs before the whips of your own men. If that is the lot you wish for, you will vote for this amendment.

[*He looks again from face to face, finally resting his gaze on* EDGAR ; *all sit with their eyes on the ground.* ANTHONY *makes a gesture, and* TENCH *hands him the book. He reads.*]

" Moved by Mr. Wilder, and seconded by Mr. Wanklin : ' That the men's demands be placed at once in the hands of Mr. Simon Harness for settlement on the lines indicated by him this morning.' " [*With sudden vigour.*] Those in favour : Signify the same in the usual way !

> [*For a minute no one moves ; then hastily, just as* ANTHONY *is about to speak,* WILDER'S *hand and* WANKLIN'S *are held up, then* SCANTLEBURY'S, *and last* EDGAR'S, *who does not lift his head.*]

Contrary ?   [ANTHONY *lifts his own hand.*]

[*In a clear voice.*] The amendment is carried.   I resign my position on this Board.

> [ENID *gasps, and there is dead silence.* ANTHONY *sits motionless, his head slowly drooping ; suddenly he heaves as though the whole of his life had risen up within him.*]

Fifty years !   You have disgraced me, gentlemen.   Bring in the men !

> [*He sits motionless, staring before him.   The Board draws hurriedly together, and forms a group.* TENCH *in a frightened manner speaks into the hall.* UNDERWOOD *almost forces* ENID *from the room.*

WILDER. [*Hurriedly*] What's to be said to them ? Why isn't Harness here ?   Ought we to see the men before he comes ?   I don't——

TENCH. Will you come in, please ?

> [*Enter* THOMAS, GREEN, BULGIN *and* ROUS, *who file up in a row past the little table.* TENCH *sits down and writes.   All eyes are fixed on* ANTHONY, *who makes no sign.*

WANKLIN. [*Stepping up to the little table, with nervous cordiality*] Well, Thomas, how's it to be ?   What's the result of your meeting ?

ROUS. Sim Harness has our answer.   He'll tell you what it is. We're waiting for him.   He'll speak for us.

WANKLIN. Is that so, Thomas ?

THOMAS. [*Sullenly*] Yes.   Roberts will not be coming, his wife is dead.

SCANTLEBURY. Yes, yes !   Poor woman !   Yes !   Yes !

FROST. [*Entering from the hall*] Mr. Harness, sir !

> [*As* HARNESS *enters he retires.*
> [HARNESS *has a piece of paper in his hand, he bows to the Directors, nods towards the men, and takes his stand behind the little table in the very centre of the room.*

HARNESS. Good evening, gentlemen.

> [TENCH, *with the paper he has been writing, joins him, they speak together in low tones.*

WILDER. We've been waiting for you, Harness.   Hope we shall come to some——

FROST. [*Entering from the hall*] Roberts.   [*He goes.*

> [ROBERTS *comes hastily in, and stands staring at* ANTHONY.   *His face is drawn and old.*

ROBERTS. Mr. Anthony, I am afraid I am a little late. I would have been here in time but for something that—has happened. [*To the men.*] Has anything been said?

THOMAS. No! But, man, what made ye come?

ROBERTS. Ye told us this morning, gentlemen, to go away and reconsider our position. We have reconsidered it; we are here to bring you the men's answer. [*To* ANTHONY.] Go ye back to London. We have nothing for you. By no jot or tittle do we abate our demands, nor will we until the whole of those demands are yielded.

> [ANTHONY *looks at him but does not speak. There is a movement amongst the men as though they were bewildered.*

HARNESS. Roberts!

ROBERTS. [*Glancing fiercely at him, and back to* ANTHONY] Is that clear enough for ye? Is it short enough and to the point? Ye made a mistake to think that we would come to heel. Ye may break the body, but ye cannot break the spirit. Get back to London, the men have nothing for ye?

> [*Pausing uneasily he takes a step towards the unmoving* ANTHONY.

EDGAR. We're all sorry for you, Roberts, but——

ROBERTS. Keep your sorrow, young man. Let your Father speak!

HARNESS. [*With the sheet of paper in his hand, speaking from behind the little table*] Roberts!

ROBERTS. [*To* ANTHONY, *with passionate intensity*] Why don't ye answer?

HARNESS. Roberts!

ROBERTS. [*Turning sharply*] What is it?

HARNESS. [*Gravely*] You're talking without the book; things have travelled past you.

> [*He makes a sign to* TENCH, *who beckons the Directors. They quickly sign his copy of the terms.*]

Look at this, man! [*Holding up his sheet of paper.*] 'Demands conceded, *with the exception of those relating to the engineers and furnace men.* Double wages for Saturday's overtime. Night-shifts as they are.' These terms have been agreed. The men go back to work again to-morrow. The strike is at an end.

ROBERTS. [*Reading the paper, and turning on the men. They shrink back from him, all but* ROUS, *who stands his ground. With deadly stillness*] Ye have gone back on me? I stood by ye to the death; ye waited for *that* to throw me over! [*The men answer, all speaking together.*

ROUS. It's a lie!

THOMAS. Ye were past endurance, man.

GREEN. If ye'd listen to me——

BULGIN. [*Under his breath*] Hold your jaw!

ROBERTS. Ye waited for *that*!

HARNESS. [*Taking the Directors' copy of the terms, and handing his own to* TENCH] That's enough, men.   You had better go.

> [*The men shuffle slowly, awkwardly away.*

WILDER. [*In a low, nervous voice*] There's nothing to stay for now, I suppose.   [*He follows to the door.*] I shall have a try for that train ! Coming, Scantlebury ?

SCANTLEBURY. [*Following with* WANKLIN] Yes, yes ; wait for me.

> [*He stops as* ROBERTS *speaks.*

ROBERTS. [*To* ANTHONY] But *ye* have not signed them terms ! They can't make terms without their Chairman !   Ye would never sign them terms !   [ANTHONY *looks at him without speaking.*] Don't tell me ye have ! for the love o' God ! [*With passionate appeal.*]   I reckoned on ye !

HARNESS. [*Holding out the Directors' copy of the terms*] The Board has signed !

> [ROBERTS *looks dully at the signatures—dashes the paper from him, and covers up his eyes.*

SCANTLEBURY. [*Behind his hand to* TENCH] Look after the Chairman !   He's not well ; he's not well—he had no lunch.   If there's any fund started for the women and children, put me down for—for twenty pounds.

> [*He goes out into the hall, in cumbrous haste ; and* WANKLIN, *who has been staring at* ROBERTS *and* ANTHONY *with twitchings of his face, follows.*   EDGAR *remains seated on the sofa, looking at the ground ;* TENCH, *returning to the bureau, writes in his minute-book.*   HARNESS *stands by the little table, gravely watching* ROBERTS.

ROBERTS. Then you're no longer Chairman of this Company ! [*Breaking into half-mad laughter.*] Ah ! ha—ah, ha, ha !   They've thrown ye over—thrown over their Chairman :   Ah—ha—ha ! [*With a sudden dreadful calm.*] So—they've done us both down, Mr. Anthony ?

> [ENID, *hurrying through the double doors, comes quickly to her father and bends over him.*

HARNESS. [*Coming down and laying his hands on* ROBERTS' *sleeve*] For shame, Roberts !   Go home quietly, man ; go home !

ROBERTS. [*Tearing his arm away*] Home ? [*Shrinking together— in a whisper.*] Home !

ENID. [*Quietly to her father*] Come away, dear !   Come to your room !

> [ANTHONY *rises with an effort.   He turns to* ROBERTS, *who looks at him.   They stand several seconds, gazing at each other fixedly ;* ANTHONY *lifts his hand, as though to salute, but lets it fall.   The expression of* ROBERTS' *face changes from hostility to wonder.   They bend their heads in token of respect.* ANTHONY

*turns, and slowly walks towards the curtained door. Suddenly
he sways as though about to fall, recovers himself and is assisted
out by* ENID *and* EDGAR, *who has hurried across the room.*
ROBERTS *remains motionless for several seconds, staring
intently after* ANTHONY, *then goes out into the hall.*

TENCH. [*Approaching* HARNESS] It's a great weight off my mind,
Mr. Harness ! But what a painful scene, sir !   [*He wipes his brow.*

    [HARNESS, *pale and resolute, regards with a grim half-smile the
quavering* TENCH.]

It's all been so violent ! What did he mean by : " Done us both
down ? " If he has lost his wife, poor fellow, he oughtn't to have
spoken to the Chairman like that !

HARNESS. A woman dead ; and the two best men both broken !

    [UNDERWOOD *enters suddenly.*

TENCH. [*Staring at* HARNESS—*suddenly excited*] D'you know, sir
—these terms, they're the *very same* we drew up together, you and I,
and put to both sides before the fight began ? All this—all this—
and—and what for ?

HARNESS. [*In a slow grim voice*] That's where the fun comes in !

    [UNDERWOOD *without turning from the door makes a gesture of
assent.*

        The curtain falls.

Notes

1   *drawing-room* — a room specifically for receiving company and to which the ladies withdraw after dinner.

1   *set out as a board table* — a table arranged to accommodate a meeting of the Directors.

1   *transfer papers* — legal papers dealing with the conveyance of property from one person to another.

1   *cadaverous* — as pale as a corpse, corpse-like.

1   *rag* — a contemptuous term denoting that the newspaper is considered worthless.

1   *Radical* — advocating the most advanced views of political reform on democratic lines.

2   *blackguarding* — speaking scurrilously about.

2   *leg-of-mutton hearts* — mutton usually eaten cold, hence cold hearted

2   *the kettle and the pot* — from the saying, 'That's the pot calling the kettle black', implying speaking derogatorily about another person while possessing the same faults (or worse) that are being criticised.

2   *capitally* — admirably.

2   *J nib* — a broad pointed nib stamped with the letter 'J'.

2   *quill* — the feather of a goose formed into a pen by pointing and slitting the lower end of the barrel.

2   *whitebait* — small silvery white fish caught in the estuary of the River Thames and elsewhere, considered a delicacy.

   read the minutes — read the record of what was said and decided at the previous meeting. Each Director would then sign them if he considered them correct.

3   *the close season* — the time of year when shooting as a sport is not allowed. It varies according to the breeding habits of the creatures concerned.

3   *E.C.* — postal district of the City of London.

3   *balance certificates* — statements showing the debit and credit sales of an account.

3   *cool their heels* — be kept waiting in order to deprive them of the impetus of the passion of the moment.

4   *fanatical* — mad as if possessed by the devil.

4   *firebrand* — one who kindles strife by inflaming passions.

5   *When we do get started we'll have to work off our contracts at the top of the market* — When the factory is producing tin plate again, it will be necessary to purchase the raw materials needed to fulfil contracts already signed. This will inevitably mean paying high prices and reducing the profit margin.

5   *playing ducks and drakes* — behaving recklessly.

6   *par* — equality between the market value and the nominal or face value.

6   *Stoic* — one of the school of Greek philosophers characterised by austerity of ethics. Name used to denote a person who practises repression of emotion, indifference to pleasure or pain and patient endurance.

6   *Better rat* — you'd better desert the cause.

6   *pig-headed* — pigs are characterised as obstinate, stupid and perverse.

7   *lantern jaw* — with long thin jaw giving a hollow appearance to the cheek.

7   *like cattle at a dog* — i.e. both defensive and aggressive as a group.

8   *claptrap* — merely a device to gain applause and intrinsically worthless.

9   *Cant!* — stock phrased repeated mechanically without meaning. Tantamount to saying: That's rubbish.

10   *plucked-looking neck* — with a neck looking long and scrawny, like a chicken's when it has been plucked.

11   *be Gad* — by God.

           Kensington — a wealthy area of London.

12   *hit below the belt* — term from boxing — an illegal and therefore dishonourable as well as painful tactic.

13   *The men will send their wives and families where the country will have to keep them* — There was no system of unemployment benefit but women and children presenting themselves at Workhouses would be given basic food and shelter paid for by the local citizens (hence, 'the country will have to keep them').

13   *We know the way the cat is jumping* — a reference to the game of 'tip-cat' in which the 'cat' — a short piece of wood tapered at both ends — is struck at one end with a stick so as to spring up and is then knocked to a distance by the same player.

14   *the ancient Trojans were fools to your father* — your father is even more foolish than the Trojans (who were responsible for their own defeat in the Trojan War). The Greeks built a wooden

horse, filled it with their best warriors and left it outside Troy.
Consumed with curiosity the Trojans hauled it into their own
city, thus admitting the enemy.

16   *the rates* — a proportion of the value of every property,
payable each year by the owner to the local government.

    old women — a derisive term used of men to imply they
are fussy and weak-willed.

17   *to throw you over* — reject your authority as Chairman by
voting against your advice.

    salver — an ornate tray used for handing refreshments,
presenting letters etc.

19   *There is a kettle on the fire* — a kettle would be boiled on a
hob on the open coal fire.

19   *her hair is not done up* — women rarely wore their hair
loose in public at this time. The fact that Annie's hair loose
indicates her state of health.

19   *sixpence* — pre-decimal currency, now worth 2½p but
more valuable then.

19   *was took* — died.

19   *a-laying' up* — lying in bed, ill and staying away from work.

19   *Compensation Acts* — Acts of 1897 and 1906 provided that
workers in some industries should be compensated by employers
for industrial accidents and disease.

20   *bread and tea* — a diet little better than bread and water.
The tea leaves would be used repeatedly to extract the last bit of
flavour.

20   *Friday's laundry job* — a part-time job in a public laundry.
All washing was done by hand or by using large coppers — it was
very hard and poorly paid work.

20   *I send Yeo out on the ice to put on the gentry's skates an'
pick up what 'e can* — Mrs. Yeo sends her husband out to earn
what he can in tips for putting on the skates of upper-class people
so that they can enjoy themselves on the frozen ponds. Very
demeaning work.

21   *the jelly* — food made by boiling and cooling vegetables or
meat, for example chicken, and then adding gelatine to make it set
into a very nutritious and easily digested form.

23   *taxes* — a compulsory contribution to the support of
government levied on persons, property, income, commodities,
transactions etc. Thus Enid's family would have to contribute far
more than Annie's.

    never touches a drop — i.e. of alcohol.

their clubs — each man would pay in a certain amount of money each week and then if he were ill or on strike, he would be entitled to some income, in this case 18 shillings. In 1900 the poverty line for a man, wife and three children was about 22 shillings.

24   *near* — niggardly, very careful with his money.

24   *pinches and stints* — restricts and limits.

26   *rowdies* — rough, disorderly people.

27   *a farthin's worth* — a farthing was the smallest unit of pre-decimal currency. There were 4 farthings in one (old) penny.

27   *the valley of the shadow of death* — variation on 'Yea, though I walk in the valley of the Shadow of Death' (Psalm 23 in the Bible).

27   *a penny whistle* — a whistle bought for one penny.

30   *blacklegs* — those willing to work for a master whose men are on strike and thus undermine the strike itself.

30   *the brand's on my soul yet* — the mark is on Harness' soul as if he had been branded like an animal.

31   *blanks* — used instead of a curse.

32   *slow-fly* — slow to react.

33   *I haf ears to my head . . . Ah! long ones!* — i.e. like a donkey renowned for its foolishness.

34   *to give us the go-by* — to outstrip and leave behind as in a race.

34   *blanky* — cursed.

34   *turned your coat* — changed your principles, allegiance.

34   *muffler* — scarf

40   *spindle-legged table* — table with long and slender legs.
       old girl — term of endearment fashionable with the upper classes at the time.

41   *funk* — state of panic caused by fear.

42   *curtained door* — It was traditional to hang curtains in the front of doors to reduce draughts.
       Cut and run — from a nautical saying meaning to cut the cable and make sail without waiting to weigh anchor, hence to rush off without any consideration for anything or anybody.

42   *6.30 train up* — i.e. to London.

43   *pantry* — a store-room for food, normally entered only by servants.

43   *Socialists* — those who support the theory and policy of Socialism, which advocates the ownership and control of factories, land, property etc. by the community as a whole and their administration or distribution in the interest of all.

44   *dumb waiter* − a piece of furniture with movable trays for holding dishes etc. Also a small lift for taking food from a kitchen on one storey of a building to a dining-room on another.

44   *disposed of her* − send her away rudely.

46   *sotto voce* − in an undertone.

46   *minute book* − official book in which records of all meetings are kept.

46   *stylographic pen* − a variety of fountain pen.

46   *General meeting* − yearly meeting of all shareholders where Directors report on the state of the Company and shareholders can make their views plain.

46   *haul us over the coals* − be extremely critical of us.

47   *Trustees* − persons appointed to manage the affiars of the Company.

48   *cock-and-bull story* − a concocted, incredible story.

48   *overshooting the mark* − going further than is proper.

49   *cut-throat policy* − a policy which involves harming others very badly, even to the extent of causing death.

49   *a coroner's jury* − in the event of a person dying by violence or accident, the local coroner holds an inquest into the circumstances of the death. A jury bring in a verdict as to the cause of death.

50   *to stand by my guns* − to maintain my position.

51   *as the poles* − as far apart as the North and South poles.

52   *like Oliver Twist* − reference to Dickens' hero, who as a child in the workhouse dared to ask for more food.

51   *bog of bankruptcy* − the involved legal proceedings and complex social results of being bankrupt.

54   *By no jot or tittle* − by not even the least part.

54   *talking without the book* − talking without authority.

55   *in cumbrous haste* − in a great hurry handicapped by excess weight.

Michael Bryant as David Roberts in the National Theatre production.

A meeting of the Directors. National Theatre production.

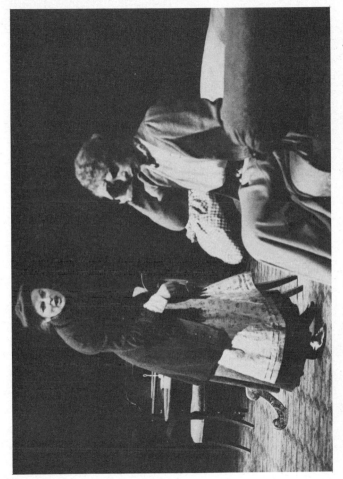

Brenda Blethyn as Madge Thomas (*left*) and Sara Kestelman as Enid Underwood.

The Trenartha Tin Plate Works as staged by the National Theatre.

Tamara Hinchco as Annie Roberts (*left*) with Sara Kestelman as Enid Underwood.

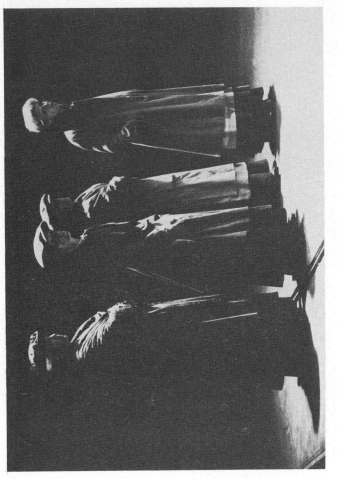

A group of workers' wives in the National Theatre production.

Christopher Morahan, the director of the National Theatre production, with the set in the background.